The iPad
PocketGuide
Third Edition

Jeff**Carlson**

Ginormous knowledge, pocket-sized.

**Peachpit
Press**

The iPad Pocket Guide, Third Edition
Jeff Carlson

Peachpit Press
1249 Eighth Street
Berkeley, CA 94710
510/524-2178
510/524-2221 (fax)

Find us on the Web at: www.peachpit.com
To report errors, please send a note to errata@peachpit.com

Peachpit Press is a division of Pearson Education.

Editor: Clifford Colby
Copyeditor: Scout Festa
Production editor: David Van Ness
Compositor: Jeff Carlson
Indexer: Valerie Haynes Perry
Cover design: Peachpit Press
Cover photography: Jeff Carlson
Interior design: Peachpit Press

ISBN-13:   978-0-321-83465-2
ISBN-10:   0-321-83465-8

9 8 7 6 5 4 3 2 1

Printed and bound in the United States of America

For Kimberly and Ellie

Acknowledgments

As I get to the end of a book project, I become more like a hermit in a cave, singularly focused on getting everything done on a tight schedule. But books can't happen in isolation, and I was fortunate enough to have these wonderful people just outside the cave entrance, waiting with positive words and, on occasion, dessert.

This book exists because of the wonderful patience and encouragement from my wife, Kim, and my daughter, Ellie.

My editor Cliff Colby shepherded the project from the beginning, while David Van Ness, Scout Festa, and Valerie Perry put their amazing talents to work to create a high-quality finished product.

Agen G. N. Schmitz updated Chapter 7 in the previous edition of this book, and I forgot to list him in the acknowledgments then. So, just in case I blank out in the future: Agen G. N. Schmitz, Agen G. N. Schmitz, Agen G. N. Schmitz. He's also been a great late-night virtual officemate as we've tackled several independent projects this year.

Several people at Apple helped with answers to my questions, including Janette Barrios, Keri Walker, Monica Sarkar, Lacey Haines, and Simon Pope.

My colleague Glenn Fleishman continues to be the best officemate, sounding board, and friend a guy could have.

Heidi Blondin and Bert Hopkins, and their son, Logan, proved to be the Best Neighbors Ever for watching Ellie at a few crucial deadline crunches.

I'd like to say I had the idea first, but Scott Knaster inspired the caption for Figure 7.18.

About Jeff Carlson

Jeff Carlson gave up an opportunity to intern at a design firm during college because they really just wanted someone tall to play on their volleyball team. In the intervening years, he's been a designer and writer, authoring best-selling books on the Macintosh, Web design, video editing, and digital photography. He's currently a columnist for the *Seattle Times* and a senior editor of *TidBITS* (www.tidbits.com), and he consumes almost too much coffee—almost. Find more information about him at jeffcarlson.com and neverenoughcoffee.com, and follow him on Twitter at @jeffcarlson.

Contents

Introduction

When the original iPad debuted two years ago (yes, it's been only two years), it seemed like a grand experiment. It was an impressive new device, but would people actually buy it? And when they did—in massive, unexpected numbers—I honestly had a hard time figuring out why. Don't get me wrong—I love the iPad and use it every day, but I'm also a nerd who writes about technology for a living. I wondered why Apple has sold more than 55 million iPads to date. And then I realized the secret to the iPad's ongoing success.

The iPad is the first real spontaneous device. It's not as bulky as a laptop, and it doesn't need to be anchored in one room of the house the way a desktop computer usually is. The iPad can be anywhere in the house, or with you on the bus or train, and is a godsend for anyone who frequently travels by air in cramped middle seats. You can pick it up and search for something—like an actor's name while watching TV—without having to relocate to "the computer" or trying to remember to look up the detail later. Heck, if you also own an Apple TV, you can play a video stored on the iPad directly on your high-definition television. You can take the iPad into the kitchen and use an app such as Epicurious to find a recipe and cook a meal.

At the same time, the iPad is not ultra compact like the iPhone. Although the iPad and iPhone share many features—they're both based on the same underlying operating system, iOS—the iPad's larger screen does make a difference when interacting with software, viewing photos, and reading electronic books (especially if you increase the text size because your eyes don't see as well as they used to).

So what is the iPad? It's all the things I mentioned, enhanced by the way you interact with it—by touch. It's the first gadget in a long, long time that really makes a huge difference to use in person rather than just read about online. The newest, third-generation iPad is thin and light, which makes a difference every time you pick it up—and, being a tablet, it's almost always in your hands when you use it. At the same time, its powerful processor and fast graphics make everything quick and responsive. You forget you're using a computer and focus on making music, watching an HD movie, reading a book, playing a game, creating a presentation, or video-chatting with remote friends and family members.

Also, this is just the beginning: Apple believes the iPad is the future of computing. The iPad is no longer tethered to a computer and can operate on its own. Data can be backed up using Apple's free iCloud service. Or, if you choose to continue to sync with a Mac or Windows PC, you can do so over a Wi-Fi network instead of using the iPad's sync cable. As someone who uses the iPad many times a day, every day, I'm inclined to agree that this is definitely a "post-PC" device.

Conventions Used in This Book

The iPad is a computer, but it introduces a few new ways of interacting with software that differ from conventions used on computers running Microsoft Windows or Mac OS X. Here's how I refer to a few things that crop up throughout the book.

Referring to iPad models

This book focuses on the third-generation iPad (introduced in March 2012)v, which Apple calls, simply, iPad. When I refer to an "iPad," in nearly all cases that's the model I'm talking about. If I need to mention earlier models, I'll refer to them as the original iPad or the iPad 2.

Popovers

It's taken me a while to not think of breakfast pastry when I type this, but a "popover" (Apple's term) is a new interface element introduced on the iPad. A popover is a floating list of options that appears when you tap some buttons (**Figure 1**).

Figure 1

A popover in Safari

Navigating settings

When I mention a system preference in the Settings app, I do so with symbols to indicate the hierarchy of taps. So, when I write *Settings > Safari > AutoFill*, that translates to:

1. At the Home screen, tap the Settings app.

2. Tap the Safari button in the left-hand pane.

3. Tap the AutoFill button in the right-hand pane.

The Action menu

Apple isn't consistent about what to call this important interface element that shows up in nearly every app. I've seen it referred to as a Share menu in apps where the options are focused on sharing, but many other apps include non-sharing commands in the menu. So, I'm sticking with the Action menu (⬆). In nearly every case, when you tap this control you're accessing commands that perform some sort of action, such as sharing, printing, copying, and the like (**Figure 2**).

Figure 2

The Action menu in the Photos app

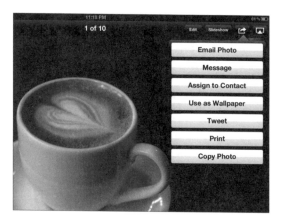

Meet the iPad

It's not often that something really new appears. Desktop and laptop computers are so commonplace, it's hard to believe that not too long ago you could go to the airport and see maybe one or two personal computers, total. The iPhone represented a new direction for Apple—and, it turns out, the cell phone industry—but it was still just a smartphone executed really well. (What's interesting is that the iPad actually came first: Apple took the work it put into developing a tablet operating system and decided to bring it to market first as a phone.)

Companies—Apple included—had tried to create tablet computers for years and failed. So what makes the iPad different? The iPad isn't the same old desktop software pressed into a laptop case that's missing a keyboard. It was designed from scratch to be a mobile tablet. And as you'll see when you use it and as you read this book, that's a profound difference. It's not a laptop replacement (although it takes that role for some people), and it's not a limited handheld device, either. The iPad shares the same underlying operating system as the iPhone, so many aspects may be familiar if you already own an iPhone or iPod touch, but it doesn't rely on old computing crutches like using a mouse pointer or forcing the user to wrangle a sprawling file system.

Instead, the iPad is a big step forward based on an old, simple idea: Anyone can take advantage of computing and digital media, without needing to be a computer expert—or even a "computer person." People shouldn't have to understand a hierarchical file system or virtual memory. This idea sounds simple, yet it's extremely difficult to do. Even after years of making computers "for the rest of us," Apple is very close to doing it.

The iPad is the first step toward a new future. I'm not talking about robots and jet packs—though you might think I sound like I've spent too much time at a high altitude—but rather a dramatic break from what we expect computers to be. And that's a truly new idea.

Power On and Set Up the iPad

An iPad doesn't require a computer at all—though one is definitely helpful to have. Apple's step-by-step getting started process is easy to follow, but you're prompted to make several decisions about how your data is synchronized and where it will live. (If you've already done this stage, skip ahead to "iPad Essentials.")

1. To power the iPad on for the first time, press and briefly hold the button at the top of the iPad until the Apple logo appears.

2. Slide the "Slide to set up" slider to get started, then choose a language and your geographic region.

3. On the Location Services screen, tap the Enable Location Services button. This option allows apps such as Maps to use data related to your whereabouts. You can choose to disable Location Services if you're concerned about privacy, but that limits the functionality of many things, such as Find My iPad. (You can enable or disable the option later in the iPad's settings, too.) Tap the Next button.

4. Tap the name of a nearby Wi-Fi network and enter its password to get online. Tap Next.   *n180prescott*

5. Choose whether to set up the device as a new iPad or to restore data from an iCloud or iTunes backup, and then tap Next.

   ■ To set up a new iPad, you'll need to enter an Apple ID (or create a new one if you don't have one). The Apple ID is what you normally use to buy media from iTunes, the App Store, or the Mac App Store.

   ■ For iCloud, you'll need to enter your iCloud user name and password.

   ■ For iTunes, you'll need to connect a sync cable between the iPad and the computer running iTunes. In iTunes, choose the name of the device you want to use as the backup source. The iPad will restart, and iTunes will sync the settings and content from the backup to it. You will then need to repeat some of the setup steps.

6. Review the Terms and Conditions for using the iPad, and agree to them by tapping the Agree button.

7. Choose whether to use iCloud to sync data using Apple's cloud service. It enables you to automatically synchronize contacts, calendars, email, photos, and documents among all of your devices, as well as optionally back up your iPad's data. Tap the Use iCloud button, and then tap Next.

8. If you want to back up your iPad's data using iCloud, tap the Back Up to iCloud button on the next screen. When the iPad is connected to a power source (whether that's a computer or just the charging plug and sync cable) and is on a Wi-Fi network, your data is copied to Apple's iCloud servers. (See "Use iCloud," later, for more information.)

   If you prefer to keep your backup local—for example, perhaps your Internet connection is metered or especially slow—tap the Back Up to My Computer button and then tap Next. Although I have a good Internet connection, I still prefer to back up to my computer because that's the easiest and fastest way to restore the data in case anything goes wrong.

9. Tap the Use Find My iPad button to enable the fantastic Find My iPad feature. This option lets you locate the iPad on a map, play an alert sound (which is handy if you know the iPad is somewhere in your house, but you can't find it), or display a message.

10. Tap the Use Dictation button to be able to dictate text. Apple needs your permission because your voice data is transmitted to the company's servers and processed there.

11. If you want Apple to receive anonymized usage data and diagnostic information in the event something crashes, tap the Automatically Send button in the Diagnostics screen. If you'd prefer not to share the data, tap Don't Send. Tap Next to continue.

12. Lastly, tap the Start Using iPad button to finish setup.

tip If you already have a lot of apps for your iPhone or iPod touch, iTunes may want to transfer them all to the iPad. Instead of deselecting unwanted apps one by one, do this: In the Apps tab in iTunes, Command-click (Mac) or Control-click (Windows) one app's checkbox to deselect them all. Then, go through the list and enable the apps you want to transfer.

note
I own an iPhone, which goes with me everywhere. Because my iPad acts as an extension of all of my important data, I chose to use the data from my iPhone instead of configuring the iPad from scratch. If you take this route, you'll still need to do some cleanup work; I found that some universal iPad apps (ones which can run on either an iPhone or the iPad) did not transfer automatically, but otherwise the process was smooth.

iPad Essentials

After the iPad is set up, and each time you press the power button or Home button, a Slide to Unlock control appears. Drag your finger left to right along the slider to advance past the opening screen.

Sleep and wake

Once powered on, the iPad rarely needs to be turned off. Instead, when you're finished using it, press the power button once (without holding it) to put it into a low-powered sleep mode.

note
The iPad automatically goes to sleep after 5 minutes of inactivity to conserve battery power. You can change that amount in the Settings app by tapping General, then Auto-Lock, and tapping a time duration (1 to 5 minutes, or Never if you want to always put the iPad to sleep manually).

To wake the iPad, press the power button or the Home button and then use the Slide to Unlock control.

Sleep and wake using a Smart Cover

Apple's Smart Covers were designed alongside the iPad: They inter-act with magnets built into the iPad's case to align the cover and also provide a nifty sleep/wake feature. Open the Smart Cover to wake the iPad, or close the cover to put the iPad to sleep. (Other companies also make cases that interact with the magnets in the same way.)

You can disable this behavior by going to Settings > General and then turning off the iPad Cover Lock/Unlock option.

Power off

It's rare that I turn off the iPad completely—usually only when something seems to be wrong and I want to restart it, or if I know I won't be using it for an extended period of time (like *that's* realistic). To do so, press and hold the power button until the red Slide to Power Off control appears. Slide it to turn off the power.

tip To prevent just anyone from unlocking your iPad and accessing your data, I highly recommend that you specify a passcode that must be entered first. See Chapter 11 for more information.

Home screen

After you've unlocked the iPad, you're taken to the Home screen, which displays the software applications (or "apps") stored on the device (**Figure 1.1**). When your iPad holds more than 20 apps, a new Home screen is created; you can see how many screens are available by looking at the dots near the bottom of the screen. Swipe left or right to switch between each screen. The shelf at the bottom of the screen holds up to six apps that remain visible on every Home screen.

tip Yes, that's right. Although the shelf holds four apps initially, you can add two more apps of your choosing.

Press the Home button in the bezel at any time to exit an app and go to the last Home screen you were viewing. If you press the button when you're already on a Home screen, you're taken to the first screen. Or, if you're currently viewing the first screen, pressing the button displays the Spotlight search page; see "Search Using Spotlight," later in this chapter.

Figure 1.1
Apps on the
Home screen

Launch and run apps

Tap once on an app's icon to launch it. (That's it. No double-clicking, pressing Command-O, or hitting Return and wondering if Windows is actually opening the program.)

Unlike most desktop or laptop computers, the iPad displays one app at a time, which takes over the entire screen; it's not possible, for example, to have Mail on one side of the screen and Safari on the other. To switch to a different app, press the Home button and then tap the other app's icon from the Home screen.

 For more information about customizing the Home screen and working with apps, see Chapter 2.

Switch quickly between apps

Even though only one app is visible at a time, the iPad runs several apps at the same time (a feature known as *multitasking*). When you exit one app, it's effectively frozen until you return to it. Some apps can continue to work in the background—Mail can send and receive messages, iPod can play music, and so forth—but most apps wait until they're activated, at which point they resume where they left off.

- To view your most recent apps, press the Home button twice quickly. (You can also swipe up with four or five fingers, but first go to Settings > General and turn on the Multitasking Gestures option. It's off by default, but I recommend enabling it.) The multitasking bar appears at the bottom of the screen (**Figure 1.2**). Flick left on the list to view more apps, and tap the app you wish to open.

- When you're viewing an app, swipe left or right with four or five fingers to switch to the next or previous app, bypassing a trip to the Home screen.

- Pinch with five fingers to return to the Home screen without pressing the physical Home button.

Figure 1.2
The multitasking bar

Change screen orientation

One of the coolest features of the iPad is the accelerometer, a sensor inside that knows how the iPad is being held, including whether the screen is in a tall (portrait) or wide (landscape) orientation. Knowing the position is important, because the iPad's operating system adjusts to the orientation: Hold the Notes app in portrait position and the screen is filled with the yellow pad; rotate the display to the landscape position and a list of notes appears to the left of the pad (**Figure 1.3**).

Figure 1.3
Screen rotation

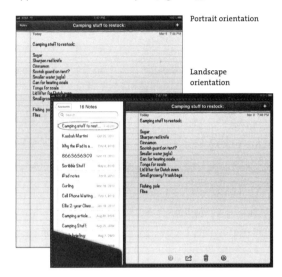

Portrait orientation

Landscape orientation

Simply turn the iPad to change its orientation. In fact, from the software's point of view, there is no "correct" orientation. No matter how you hold it, the screen contents rotate to be right-side up.

Screen orientation is just a parlor trick for the accelerometer, however. Because it calculates the iPad's position in three dimensions, it also knows at what angle you're holding the device and responds to that. Plus, a built-in gyroscope and compass make it possible for the iPad to calculate where it's being held in physical space. Many games take advantage of these features, turning the entire iPad into the game controller to affect what's happening onscreen.

Lock screen rotation

You may not want the screen to adjust its orientation at times, like when you're reading while lying down. The iPad offers two ways to do this: The iPad side switch, located next to the volume adjustment button, can be set to lock the orientation or to mute audio; or, you can tap a control in the multitasking bar.

tip When the side switch is configured to lock screen orientation, you can still easily mute the iPad's audio: Press and hold the volume-down button for a couple of seconds. The volume level dips and then drops to zero.

To choose which behavior to use, you need to specify how the iPad side switch is used:

1. Open the Settings app and tap the General setting.

2. Under the "Use Side Switch to" heading, tap to choose either Lock Rotation or Mute.

   Based on your choice here, the opposite action becomes the option available in the multitasking bar.

To lock screen orientation or mute the iPad volume using the multitasking bar, do the following:

1. Double-press the Home button to reveal the multitasking bar.

2. Swipe left-to-right to reveal a set of system-wide controls (**Figure 1.4**).

3. Tap the left-most button to either lock orientation or mute audio, depending on the side switch setting.

Figure 1.4
Lock orientation in the multi-tasking bar

Orientation Lock button

Adjust screen brightness

Normally, the iPad's ambient-light sensor adjusts the screen brightness automatically according to its surroundings. If you'd like to dim the light or punch it up manually, you can do so in two places:

- Go to Settings > Brightness & Wallpaper and drag the slider left (darker) or right (brighter). To always adjust manually, turn off the Auto-Brightness switch.

- Double-press the Home button to bring up the multitasking bar, swipe right, and adjust the brightness slider (located just to the left of the audio playback controls).

Charge the iPad battery

The iPad includes a non-removable lithium-polymer battery that provides up to 10 hours of use on a single charge. (In fact, Apple claims that 10 hours of video playback, surfing the Web using Wi-Fi, or listening to music are possible.) You can check the state of the battery by looking at the indicator in the upper-right corner of the screen (**Figure 1.5**).

Figure 1.5
Battery indicator

Current battery charge

 To show or hide the percentage next to the battery indicatory, go to Settings > General > Usage and tap the Battery Percentage switch.

Actual battery life depends on how you use the iPad, of course—playing a video game that makes extensive use of 3D graphics is more demanding on the processor and will eat up power faster than reading a book in iBooks. As the battery nears depletion, warning messages appear when

20 percent and 10 percent of the power remains. After that, the iPad becomes unresponsive and needs to be charged to function again.

To replenish the battery's charge, plug the iPad's sync cable into the included power adapter (charging takes about four hours if the battery is nearly spent).

You can also plug the sync cable into your computer to sync and recharge, but there's a catch: Your computer's USB port may not have the oomph to do it. If that's the case, you'll see "Not Charging" in the power indicator at the upper-right corner of the screen.

The specifications for running power over USB call for at least 5V (volts), but the iPad requires more than that. Some computers, such as recent Apple laptops and desktops, can optionally provide as much as 12V when a device that requires it is connected. In that case, the iPad will charge, but more slowly than when connected to the power adapter. The upside is that when the iPad is connected to a low-power USB port, the battery does not deplete; in fact, it will trickle-charge slowly when the iPad is asleep, and keep a steady level when it's awake.

Conserve battery life

You can take steps to make the most of the battery's charge. No need to be slavish about these, but you'll definitely want to implement them when you get a low battery notice:

- Turn down the screen brightness.
- Turn off Wi-Fi if you're not within range of a wireless network.
- Turn off Bluetooth if you're not using it.
- Disable notifications.
- Disable cellular networking (provided you own the 4G model) if you're not accessing data online (discussed later in this chapter).

What if the battery dies?

Batteries lose capacity over time, but sometimes a battery won't hold a charge for nearly as long as it once did. If the iPad is still under warranty (one year, or two years if you also purchased AppleCare for it), contact Apple and ask for a replacement iPad. If an Apple retail store is nearby, an Apple Genius will be able to diagnose whether the battery is faulty.

If you're out of warranty and the iPad "requires service due to the battery's diminished ability to hold an electrical charge" (in Apple's words), then you can take advantage of Apple's battery replacement service. For $99, Apple will replace the entire iPad (so be sure you've synchronized it before sending it off). See www.apple.com/support/ipad/service/battery/ for more information.

Multi-Touch Gestures

You probably noticed that when you opened the iPad's box, no stylus fell out. Until recently, most tablet computers and handhelds required that you use a plastic pencil to do anything. The iPad, instead, is designed for your fingers. You interact with the software on the screen by touching, tapping, swiping, and performing other Multi-Touch gestures. Many controls are intuitive: Tap the Edit button in Contacts, for example, to edit a person's information. Other motions may not be obvious at first, but they quickly become natural.

Tap

As you've no doubt discovered, the most obvious action is to point at an area of the screen, like a button or other control, and lightly tap with one finger. Sometimes, you'll want to double-tap the screen, such as when you want to zoom in on a section of a Web page in Safari.

When you encounter an On/Off switch, you can slide the switch if you want, or simply tap it to change its state.

Touch and hold

Instead of quickly tapping and lifting your finger from the screen, there are times when you want to touch the screen and maintain contact to elicit an action (for example, see "Work with Text," ahead).

Drag

Touch and hold a point on the screen, then move your finger across the glass. Drag a Web page in Safari from bottom to top to scroll as you read.

Flick and swipe

A flick (yes, that's Apple's official name for it) is like a drag, but faster. On a Web page, touch the screen and flick your finger to "throw" the page in any direction. The software simulates the physics of the motion and slows the scrolling page until it comes to a stop, based on the velocity of the flick.

A swipe is similar to a flick, but you drag something (usually horizontally) a bit more slowly. You swipe a photo from right to left to advance to the next picture, for instance.

 The iPad's screen responds to the electricity in your fingers, not to pressure. Pressing harder on the display doesn't improve its response.

Pinch

When you want to zoom in or out on an item, such as a map, a photo, or a Web page, touch two fingers to the screen and pinch them together (to zoom out) or spread them apart (to zoom in).

Rotate

Press two fingers to the screen and rotate them in a circle to rotate something, such as a photo in the Photos app.

Shake

Yes, that's right, give the iPad a good shake. The accelerometer recognizes the motion as an intentional vibration, and software that's been written to handle the gesture can act on it. For example, when you're typing in the Notes app and make a mistake, shake the iPad to bring up a dialog that gives you the option to undo the last action. I've found that shaking front to back, not side to side, seems to be more responsive.

Use two hands

The iPad's entire screen is filled with sensors, so take advantage of the large display area and use both hands. One obvious application is the keyboard that appears when you're entering text; since it's nearly full size, you can type as you would on a physical keyboard.

For another example, look to Apple's Keynote app: Touch and hold a slide with the finger of one hand, and then use your other hand to tap other slides to select them all in a group. Numerous games and other apps also accept two-handed input.

Work with Text

It's one thing to view photos and movies, but how do you enter and edit text? Whether you're typing a Web address, adding an event to your calendar, or composing a letter, you need to know how to put letters to screen. You'll encounter the following basic operations throughout the iPad environment.

Type text

Whenever you tap an editable text area, the iPad's software keyboard slides up from the bottom of the screen (**Figure 1.6**). Type on it as you would a regular keyboard, keeping a few things in mind:

- The screen can't accommodate a full-sized keyboard, so some characters appear where you may not expect them. For example, you type an exclamation point (!) by holding the Shift (⟨⇧⟩) key and tapping the comma (,) key. Number keys are accessed by tapping the ".?123" key, and symbols such as the equals sign (=) are available after next tapping the "#+=" key.

Figure 1.6

The onscreen keyboard

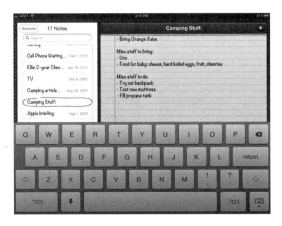

- The keyboard varies depending on the context of the text field. When you're in the Address field in Safari, you'll see a ".com" key—a shortcut for the often-typed end to a Web address—and the Return key reads "Go." At other times, you may not see letters at all, such as when a number keypad and options for different functions appear when you edit values in Numbers.

tip To quickly enter other domain name suffixes, like .net or .org, touch and hold the ".com" key. A pop-up menu presents other options for you to tap to add to the text. The same is true for typing accented characters.

- To hide the keyboard without exiting the text field, tap the ⌨ key.

- You can end a sentence with a period by simply tapping two spaces after a word. (This shortcut came about on the iPhone, where the period key doesn't appear on the first screen of keys.) If you'd rather turn off this feature, go to Settings > General > Keyboard and disable the "." Shortcut option.

tip Want to know the most useful iPad keyboard tip? To type an apostrophe, which isn't on the main screen, touch the comma (,) key and slide your finger up to insert the apostrophe character. You can do the same with the period (.) key to get a double-quotation mark.

- By default, the Caps Lock feature is disabled (nobody likes it when PEOPLE SHOUT, after all), but if you often type acronyms or otherwise want the option, go to Settings > General > Keyboard and turn on the Enable Caps Lock option. When typing, quickly double-tap the Shift key to enter Caps Lock mode; the face of the key is highlighted (versus just the up-arrow icon when normal Shift is active).

note If you look closely at the software keyboard, you'll see faux raised bumps on the F and J keys, which on a physical keyboard help touch-typists determine their finger position without looking at the keys. There's no raised portion of glass on the screen, of course, but it's a subtle visual clue, meant to make you feel more at home typing on the smooth surface. All sorts of little "real-world" touches like this one are scattered throughout the iPad interface.

Split or move the keyboard

When you're holding the iPad, versus resting it on a flat surface, how do you type? Balanced on one hand and typing with the other hand?

With your thumbs, like on a smartphone? I fall in the latter camp, and my fingers are just barely long enough to accommodate the onscreen keyboard when the iPad is in its portrait orientation.

To make it easier for people to type, Apple introduced a new split-keyboard option in iOS 5. The keys can also be repositioned vertically on the screen.

1. In an app that accepts text input, tap to place the cursor and bring up the onscreen keyboard.

2. Drag the right edge of the ⌨ key up the screen; as you drag, the keyboard splits (**Figure 1.7**).

3. To position the split keyboard higher on the screen, continue dragging up.

Figure 1.7
The split keyboard

To return the keyboard back to its original, joined state, drag the ⌨ key back to the bottom of the screen.

Auto-Correction

This extremely helpful feature debuted on the iPhone, where the smaller screen size makes it more challenging to hit the right keys as you're typing. As you type, the iPad analyzes your letters to look for patterns and offers suggestions in a little pop-up box (**Figure 1.8**). To accept the suggestion, type a space or punctuation. To ignore it, either tap the X on the pop-up or continue typing letters. (Also see "Cut, Copy, Paste, and Suggest," just ahead.)

Figure 1.8
Text auto-correction

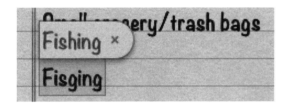

If the feature is getting in your way, go to Settings > General > Keyboard. While there, you can also disable Auto-Capitalization, which automatically enables the Shift key after you've applied punctuation.

Shortcuts

If you frequently type the same phrases, you can set up shortcuts that expand to longer items. For example, instead of writing "Cheers! Jeff" at the end of every email message, I could set up a shortcut of "cjf" to insert that text for me.

1. Go to Settings > General > Keyboard, and tap Add New Shortcut.

2. Type the text you want expanded in the Phrase field.

3. Type the shortcut text in the Shortcut field.

4. Tap the Save button.

Select text

On a computer, selecting text is easy: You position your mouse pointer, then click and drag to select the text you want. The iPad has no mouse pointer, so the process of selecting text is slightly different.

1. Within any range of text (not just in text-entry fields), touch and hold where you want to start selecting. A magnified view of the area appears above your finger (**Figure 1.9**).

Figure 1.9
*Select text with
magnification.*

2. Position the insertion point and release your finger. As you'll see in a moment, you don't need to put the insertion point at the exact start of your selection.

3. In the pop-up that appears, choose Select to highlight the closest word; or, tap Select All to highlight a full sentence.

4. Drag the handles to the left and right of the initial selection to define the full area you wish to select (**Figure 1.10**). If you drag beyond a paragraph, the selection area broadens to include blocks of text instead of letter-by-letter selections.

Figure 1.10
*Drag to
highlight text.*

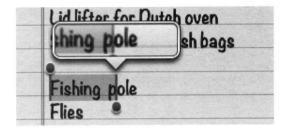

tip   If you're in an editable text area (versus a read-only area like a Web page), double-tap a word to select it. Or, tap four times quickly to select an entire sentence. Or, here's a quick tip that doesn't apply just to editable areas: Double-tap a word, but hold the second tap to make a selection, and then drag to expand it without lifting your finger.

note   Selecting text occasionally works differently depending on which app you're using. In Safari, for example, touching and holding on text on a Web page selects whichever word is under your finger; drag to select any word, lift your finger, and then expand the selection.

Cut, Copy, Paste, and Suggest

When you make a selection, a set of options appears above the text.

- **Cut:** The selection is copied to memory and then removed from the content you're editing.

- **Copy:** The selected content is just copied to memory.

- **Paste:** If you've previously cut or copied some text, the Paste option appears. Tap Paste to add the content stored in memory; if a selection is made, the pasted content overwrites the selection.

- **Suggest:** Does a word look misspelled? Select it and tap the Suggest button. If the iPad comes up with a different spelling (or a similar word), it appears in a pop-up—tap the suggestion to replace the selected word (**Figure 1.11**).

Figure 1.11
Selection options

After choosing the Suggest option

Misspelled words also appear with a dotted red underline. Tap once on the word to view suggestions (**Figure 1.12**).

Figure 1.12
A misspelled word underlined

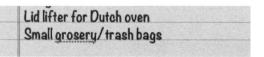

tip Selecting, copying, and pasting aren't reserved solely for text. In Safari, for example, you can select a range of text that also includes an image, copy it, and then open Mail and paste the formatted content into an outgoing message.

Voice dictation

The third-generation iPad didn't get one of the signature features of the iPhone 4S—the Siri voice-activated personal assistant—but it did gain access to part of Siri's technology: voice dictation. If you're more comfortable speaking instead of typing on the iPad's keyboard, definitely give voice dictation a try; I'm regularly amazed at the quality of the transcription.

1. Tap any text field (such as the Messages app) to make the onscreen keyboard appear.

2. Tap the Voice Dictation button (**Figure 1.13**).

3. Speak the text you'd like to type. Remember to speak punctuation, like "period" or "question mark," to include it. For example, to type *Robert, did you remember to buy groceries?*, you'd say, "Robert comma did you remember to buy groceries question mark."

4. Tap the Done button, or pause long enough for the iPad to guess that you're finished.

Figure 1.13
The Voice Dictation button during dictation

Sync with a Computer

Although an iPad can do everything you need it to do by itself, chances are your music, movies, and other data reside on a Mac or Windows PC. A computer is also the easiest way to keep a backup of the iPad's data. iCloud backup is great, but it isn't appropriate for all situations (namely, when you don't have robust Internet connectivity).

The iPad's home base is iTunes, Apple's media hub software. If you don't have the latest version, go to www.apple.com/itunes/ to download and install it.

When you connect the iPad using the USB cable, the iPad appears in the iTunes sidebar. Select it to view information and options for synchronizing your data (**Figure 1.14**).

Figure 1.14

The iPad in iTunes

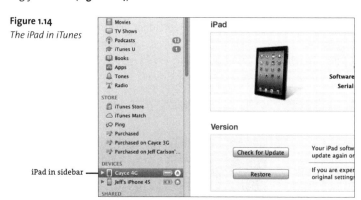

iPad in sidebar ——

note You'll be surprised at just how infrequently you may need to sync the iPad. Using iCloud, for example, you can wirelessly sync your calendars and contacts. Application updates are also available using the included App Store app (see Chapter 2).

Here's what gets transferred when you connect the iPad:

- Any new or changed data, which is added to the backup of the iPad on your computer

- Personal information such as calendars and contacts (unless you're syncing over the air; see Chapter 10)

- New and updated apps (those downloaded on the iPad and in iTunes)

- Music, movies, and TV shows

- Podcasts

- iTunes U (university courses available via iTunes)

- Photos

- Files used by iPad apps

Disconnect the iPad

When you want to take the iPad somewhere, simply disconnect the sync cable. Unlike other USB devices, the iPad doesn't need to be ejected first.

If This Is Your First Sync

The first time you connect the iPad to your computer, iTunes performs an initial sync and gives you the option to transfer your entire music and video library (space permitting). If there isn't enough room, you can choose which items are copied over. See Chapter 8.

If you already own an iPad, iPhone, or iPod touch, any apps you've purchased are automatically transferred to the iPad. However, that means *all* apps you own, including ones not currently installed on a device; the apps still reside in iTunes. Depending on the number of apps, this situation may mean just a few more minutes during the initial sync. If you've gone app-crazy, you may want to cancel the sync: Click the cancel button (⊗) in the iTunes status display. Then manually choose which apps are transferred within the Applications tab. (You don't have to click every box individually. To deselect all apps, Command-click on the Mac or Control-click under Windows.) See "Find and Install Apps" in Chapter 2 for more details.

Set up Wi-Fi sync

If you ask me, one of the best unheralded features of the iPad (and any device running iOS 5) is the ability to sync wirelessly. As long as your iPad is on the same Wi-Fi network as the computer to which you sync, you can leave that 30-pin USB cable in a drawer or use it on a bedside table for charging. Here's how to set it up:

1. Connect the iPad to the computer using the sync cable.

2. Select the iPad in the sidebar in iTunes.

3. On the Summary screen, scroll down to the Options section and select "Sync with this iPad over Wi-Fi."

4. Click the Apply button.

Whenever the iPad is plugged into power and on the Wi-Fi network, a sync operation occurs. You can also initiate a manual sync from the iPad: Open Settings > General > iTunes Wi-Fi Sync, and tap the Sync Now button.

note Even if Wi-Fi sync is enabled, the iPad will still sync when connected via the USB cable. If you're transferring a lot of data, the cable is a much faster option.

Special sync options

Synchronization mostly concerns transferring your media and related files. These options, found on the Summary screen, refine how iTunes handles the sync.

■ **Open iTunes when this iPad is connected:** Select this option to launch iTunes if it's not running when you plug in the iPad.

- **Sync only checked songs and videos:** In iTunes, you can uncheck a song's checkbox to prevent it from playing (such as when you like every song on an album except one). If this option is deselected, all songs and movies are copied to the iPad, taking up more memory.

- **Prefer standard definition videos:** Although the iPad can play Apple's HD videos, they take up much more memory. Select this option to transfer standard-definition versions of movies to conserve storage.

- **Convert higher bit rate songs to [128/192/256] kbps AAC:** Selecting this option can significantly reduce the amount of space your music collection occupies by making lower- (but still decent-) quality versions of songs: 128 kbps, 192 kbps, or 256 kbps. If you've ripped your own music at higher bit rates, choose a quality level to eke out some space on the iPad.

- **Manually manage music and videos:** Wield more control over what gets transferred to the iPad. When this option is selected, you can drag songs and videos from your iTunes library to the iPad name in the sidebar. If you decide to turn off this feature later, however, your music and videos are erased and replaced according to the options you set up in each media tab.

- **Configure Universal Access:** Click this button to enable options that make the iPad more usable for people with impaired vision or hearing. These controls mirror those found in Settings > General > Accessibility.

- **Encrypt local backup:** The data on the iPad is encrypted—scrambled so that if the iPad is lost or stolen, its contents can't be read. The backup stored on your computer's hard disk, however, is not encrypted. To make it inaccessible to prying eyes, activate this option, which is listed in the Backup section of the Summary screen when "Back up to this computer" is selected. A dialog appears, asking you to define a password and verify it.

tip What if you want to connect the iPad to your computer but don't want to sync? You can't change the automatic sync preference without the iPad connected. Instead, press and hold Command-Option (Mac) or Shift-Control (Windows) when you connect the iPad, and hold them until the iPad appears in the sidebar. It won't sync.

Update the system software

When Apple releases updates to the iOS, iTunes informs you with an alert. You can also click the Check for Update button on the Summary screen to query manually. If an update is available, you're given the option of down-loading and installing it.

On the iPad itself, you can check for updates by going to Settings > General > Software Update.

tip If you say yes to the update in iTunes, you get to choose whether to download and install it right away or just download the software for later. The second option is good if you want to take advantage of a robust Internet connection (for example, you're at the office or in a coffee shop with your laptop) but plan to update the iPad at another time (when you get home).

Connect to the Internet Using Wi-Fi

Every iPad supports Wi-Fi wireless networking, enabling you to connect to the Internet using nearby access points; you may have a Wi-Fi network set up in your house or office, or you might go to a nearby "hotspot," usually a coffee shop or restaurant. A Wi-Fi network usually covers the space of a house or small building. Compare that to 4G cellular wireless (more on that shortly), which is designed to offer miles of coverage.

Once the iPad is connected to a Wi-Fi network, you can browse the Web, send and receive email, view maps, and perform other tasks that require an Internet connection. Wi-Fi also lets you interact with other devices and computers sharing the network connection; for example, you can play a game against another iPad owner or control music playback of a computer running iTunes.

Choose a Wi-Fi access point

When the iPad requires an Internet connection, such as for accessing email or a Web page, it checks to see if an active Wi-Fi network is within range. A dialog appears with a list of nearby networks (**Figure 1.15**). Tap the name of a network you want to join, type its password if required, and then tap the Join button on the keyboard.

Figure 1.15
Available Wi-Fi networks

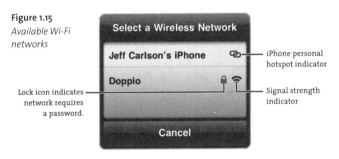

Select a Wireless Network

Jeff Carlson's iPhone — iPhone personal hotspot indicator

Lock icon indicates network requires a password. — Doppio — Signal strength indicator

Cancel

note Many public Wi-Fi hotspots don't require a password to join the network but do need you to log in using a Web form once you're connected. After you get onto the network, go to Safari and enter any valid Web address. A login page should appear if you need to sign in (or pay) for access.

tip If you'd rather not be interrupted by a pop-up list of networks, go to Settings > Wi-Fi and then turn off the Ask to Join Networks option.

tip Exercise good judgment when joining open, unprotected Wi-Fi networks. It's possible (and easy, for those who are savvy) to intercept the data passing between the iPad and the base station running the network. A nefarious network owner—or even someone at the next table in a coffee shop—could collect the data stream and mine it for things like passwords and credit card numbers. Unless you can vouch for the network owner, avoid paying bills or making purchases on public networks. See Chapter 11 for more information.

Connect to a Wi-Fi network manually

The iPad is helpful in displaying and connecting to available Wi-Fi networks, but there are times when you will want to link up with one manually—when you accidentally connected to the wrong network or the owner has hidden the network name for security, for instance. Here's how to connect using the Settings app (**Figure 1.16**).

Figure 1.16
Connect to Wi-Fi in Settings.

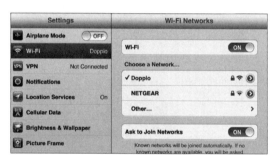

1. Tap Settings > Wi-Fi.

2. From the list that appears under Choose a Network, tap a network name.

3. If a password is required, type it into the Password field and then tap the Join button.

The network name gains a checkbox, and a Wi-Fi signal strength icon appears in the upper-left corner of the screen.

To connect to a network that isn't broadcasting its name, or if the iPad isn't listing the one you expect, do the following (**Figure 1.17**):

Figure 1.17
Join a hidden Wi-Fi network.

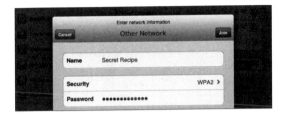

1. In the Wi-Fi screen, tap the Other button.

2. Type the network name in the Name field.

3. Tap the Security button and specify which type of encryption the network is using. If you don't know, try WPA2 first, followed by WEP (which is older and no longer secure, but still widely used).

4. Enter the network's password in the Password field that appears.

5. Tap Join to establish a connection.

tip The iPad remembers Wi-Fi network names and settings, so the next time you're within range of a network you've previously joined, a connection is automatically made.

Disconnect from a Wi-Fi network

If you accidentally join the wrong network, it's easy to sever the connection. In Settings > Wi-Fi, tap the detail button (⊙) and then tap Forget this Network.

Turn off Wi-Fi

Go to Settings > Wi-Fi and set the Wi-Fi switch to Off. You may want to do this when conserving battery power or if you're in an area where you know a Wi-Fi network isn't available.

Use a Cellular Data Network with a Wi-Fi iPad

Instead of purchasing an iPad with Wi-Fi and 4G, some people are employing a different technique to provide ubiquitous Internet access.

The Novatel Wireless MiFi (www.novatelwireless.com) is a portable Wi-Fi hotspot that connects to a cellular data network. It's pocket-sized and offers the same type of always-on connection that the iPad 4G provides. However, it's not bound to one carrier, and it can let more than one device connect at a time.

The monthly service costs more than the iPad 4G's setup, but you're not tied to Apple's preferred carriers. If you need to connect several devices over Wi-Fi (like the iPad, an iPhone, and a laptop) or can't get good reception using your cellular provider, something like the MiFi may be perfect.

If you already own an iPhone 4 or later, another option is available. For a monthly fee to your cellular service provider, you can set up the iPhone as a portable hotspot, connecting up to five devices via Wi-Fi.

Connect to the Internet Using Cellular Data

For people who tend to travel more or who need more frequent access to the Internet than is afforded by Wi-Fi hotspots, Apple offers an iPad model with 4G cellular data access built in, the same network used by modern cell phones. With 4G enabled, your iPad likely has Internet access nearly everywhere.

note The iPad can hop onto a cellular network, but it can't place or receive calls like an iPhone. The cellular access is strictly for data. (But you can still place calls using a Voice-over-IP service such as Skype.)

However, 4G is more expensive: The 4G iPad model costs $130 more than the Wi-Fi–only model in the United States and requires an additional fee to access the network. The good news is that Apple negotiated great deals with AT&T and Verizon Wireless to provide 4G access. (I'm using the U.S. carriers as the examples here, but companies worldwide also offer the iPad with 4G access. Check with your carrier for specific pricing.)

note The AT&T and Verizon iPad models require different communications hardware to connect to their networks. Be sure you purchase the correct model if you haven't done so already.

Here's how it works for AT&T customers: For $14.99, you can transfer—both downloads and uploads—250 megabytes (MB) of data within a 30-day period. For $30, you get 3 GB of data transfer during the same period; $50 pays for 5 GB of data. If you use more than your allotment, you can pay for more data. The least expensive plan for Verizon customers is $30, but that counts for 2 GB of data; other prices include $50 for 5 GB of data and $80 for 10 GB. (These prices are current as of March 2012 and may have changed by the time you read this.)

The great part of these deals is that, unlike with the iPhone, there's no contract that locks you in for a minimum length of time. Activate the plan when you need it (if you expect to travel a lot next month, for instance), and cancel when you're done. If you bump against the limit of one plan, you can jump to another plan or wait until the 30-day cycle begins again.

And you do it all from the iPad directly.

tip The 4G iPad boasts a few other differences from the Wi-Fi model. It includes a GPS chip for identifying the iPad's position in Maps and other apps; the Wi-Fi model uses a method based on wireless access points to determine its location. Also, when an AT&T 4G plan is active in the United States, you get free Wi-Fi access at AT&T-operated Wi-Fi hotspots, such as those in Starbucks, McDonalds, and many airports. The Verizon model, at least at the time of this writing, also offers the Personal Hotspot feature (see "Share the Internet connection using Portable Hotspot," a few pages ahead).

Understand 4G LTE

The idea of "4G" cellular service is as much a marketing term as a description of technology, so here's a quick overview of the iPad's 4G capabilities. My apologies in advance for the alphabet soup here.

The iPad 4G model is capable of LTE (a meaningless acronym for Long Term Evolution) data transfer, which can achieve up to 72 megabits per second (Mbps). If you're in a service area that offers LTE, that's the theoretical fastest transfer rate.

The 4G model also supports three other varieties of cellular data: DC-HSDPA (42 Mbps), HSPA+ (21 Mbps), and HSPA (7.2 Mbps). To put these into context, the iPad 2 and iPhone 4 use HSPA, and the iPhone 4S uses a slightly slower variant of HSPA+.

However, don't fret too much about these levels: The iPad 4G will connect to the best signal that's available in your area, and fall back to 3G service if necessary. As it is, LTE is currently limited to a couple of handfuls of major markets, so many iPad owners may not get to sample higher speeds unless they're on a business trip to one of those areas.

Activate cellular service

To enable cellular service, do the following:

1. Go to Settings > Cellular Data and make sure the Cellular Data option is set to On (**Figure 1.18**).

Figure 1.18
Cellular Data preferences

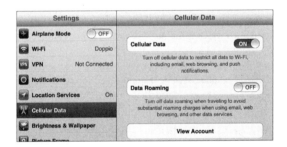

2. Tap the View Account button.

3. Enter your user information.

4. Enter login information. This is a new account for the iPad, not an existing account with your provider. (So even if you have an iPhone account, the iPad is separate.) Type an email address and a new password.

5. Tap a plan to choose it.

6. Enter your credit card and billing information and tap Next.

7. Read the terms of service and tap Agree.

8. Review the payment summary and tap Done.

After a few minutes, a dialog appears informing you that your data plan has been successfully activated.

Once cellular service is activated, you can access the Internet anywhere you have cellular reception.

Measure your cellular data usage

So, just how far will you get with 250 MB of data? As you might expect, that depends on your use. Go to Settings > General > Cellular Data > View Account. The Account Overview section tells you how much data you've used, how much remains, and how many days are left in the billing period.

note In an area where both Wi-Fi and cellular work, Wi-Fi supersedes the cellular network. Using the iPad at a Wi-Fi hotspot, for example, doesn't count toward the data limit even if cellular service is active.

Add or cancel cellular service

As you approach the end of the allotted bandwidth on the 250 MB plan, the iPad displays warnings when you reach 20 percent of data left, then 10 percent, and then zero. At any point, if you want to add bandwidth, tap the Now button to bring up the Cellular Data Account window. You can also get there at any time by going to Settings > Cellular Data and tapping Add Data or Change Plan.

note International roaming data rates can be substantially higher than what your domestic carrier offers, so if you know you'll be traveling out of the country, tap the Add International Plan button and set up a plan.

Share the Internet connection using Portable Hotspot

The iPad is capable of acting like a portable Wi-Fi hotspot, sharing its cellular Internet access with up to five devices (such as your computer or a friend's iPad). The catch is that your cellular provider may not allow it. In the United States, AT&T did not offer this Portable Hotspot feature at launch (but it was "considering" it—likely for an extra fee, as with iPhone tethering), while Verizon not only includes the feature, but also doesn't charge extra. The connection can be shared via Wi-Fi, USB, or Bluetooth.

1. Go to Settings > General > Network, and tap Set Up Personal Hotspot. After you enable the feature, a Portable Hotspot option appears on the first Settings screen.

2. Tap Portable Hotspot to view the settings, and then switch the feature to On.

3. On devices that want to connect, point them to the hotspot name (if sharing using Wi-Fi) and enter the password you set up in step 1.

tip The SIM card included with the AT&T iPad 4G model stores your name and account information. You can remove it from the iPad and put it into another device that accepts a Micro SIM card and still use your account. It ships with a PIN code that's set by the network provider. To lock the SIM card for added security, tap the SIM PIN button in the Cellular Data settings, switch SIM PIN to On, and enter 1111 (the default for AT&T in the U.S.). To set a new code, tap Change PIN and follow the instructions. (If you enter the wrong passcode three times, the SIM will be shut down and you'll need to contact the cellular provider to re-activate it. See http://support.apple.com/kb/HT4113 for more information.)

Use iCloud

iCloud is Apple's ambitious, ubiquitous service for keeping all of your data in sync no matter which computer or iOS device you're using. When you update some piece of information, such as an event in the Calendar app, the changes are copied to the iCloud servers and applied to every device that shares your iCloud account. You don't need to sync using a cable or via Wi-Fi; as long as you have a connection to the Internet, the information is updated automatically.

This feature is especially helpful when editing documents in apps that support iCloud. The process of moving a word processing document in Apple's Pages application from the computer to the iPad is cumbersome and requires a trip through iTunes. With iCloud, the file is copied wirelessly without fuss.

iCloud can sync email, contacts, calendar events, iOS reminders, Safari bookmarks, notes, music, and documents. For images, Photo Stream is a way to share new photos you capture using the iPad's camera, or to view photos you shoot with an iPhone or iPod touch or that are saved in compatible photo applications such as iPhoto.

Set up iCloud

If you didn't enable iCloud when you first set up your iPad, do the following:

1. Open Settings > iCloud.

2. Enter your Apple ID and password.

3. Tap the Sign In button. The iPad verifies the information.

4. In the dialog that appears, allow iCloud to use location information for your iPad.

The iCloud settings include On/Off switches for the types of data that can be synced (**Figure 1.19**). Tap to enable or disable any of them. For the Photo Stream and the Documents & Data options, tapping their names brings up additional options. (For example, Documents & Data lets you turn off cellular access for documents so you don't inadvertently chew up your cellular bandwidth allotment.)

Figure 1.19
iCloud settings

Sync data to iCloud

The beauty of iCloud is that once it's enabled, you don't have to do much else. Contacts and calendars, for instance, are automatically updated. Some items require a small amount of manual intervention. For example, music, TV shows, or apps you've purchased from the iTunes Store on a separate device can be downloaded to the iPad (see Chapter 8).

tip An option in iTunes lets you download new music, apps, or books to all of your devices when you purchase them. Go to iTunes > Preferences, tap the Store icon, and turn on the Automatic Downloads options for the media you want.

note You can access your contacts, calendars, email, and iWork documents using any modern Web browser at www.icloud.com.

iCloud backup

Instead of backing up the iPad's data to iTunes, you can back it up directly to iCloud when the iPad is connected to a Wi-Fi network and being charged. Go to Settings > iCloud > Storage & Backup and enable the iCloud Backup option. (You can also choose "Back up to iCloud" in iTunes on the iPad's Summary screen.) Here you can also see how much of your free 5 GB capacity is being used. As you might guess, Apple is happy to sell you more storage space.

Click the Manage Storage button to view which items are being stored and how much space they occupy. Some types of data stored on your iPad don't count against the 5 GB of free storage, such as Photo Stream images and purchased music, apps, books, and TV shows.

Read Notifications

Under previous versions of iOS, notifications were a hassle. If an app put up a notice—for example, I use Boxcar (www.boxcar.io) to alert me when I receive Facebook or Twitter direct messages—it appeared as a solitary box, obscuring everything else. iOS 5 revamped notifications, making them much more useful.

You can read notifications by doing one of the following:

- Swipe down with one finger from the top of the screen to view the Notifications drawer (**Figure 1.20**). Tap an item to go directly to it in the appropriate app. To hide the drawer, drag it back to the top of the screen.

- When a notification arrives as a dialog, swipe the icon next to the message to jump directly to that app (**Figure 1.21**).

- When you're using the iPad, a new notification appears in a banner at the top of the screen. Tap it to view its app.

Figure 1.20
Notifications drawer

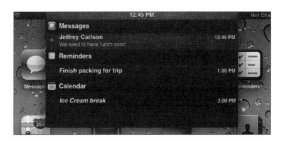

Figure 1.21
A Messages notification as a dialog

> **tip** Customize the appearance of notifications (such as whether new alerts show up as a banner at the top of the screen, show up as a dialog, or do not show up at all) by going to Settings > Notifications.

> **tip** The banner notifications are mostly unintrusive, but sometimes they do get in the way. To quickly dismiss one, swipe down and back up over the banner quicky.

Connect to Bluetooth Devices

The iPad includes just two ports for connecting cables: the headphone port at the top and the dock port at the bottom. The rest of the iPad's communication happens wirelessly via Wi-Fi, cellular, or a third option: Bluetooth. Thanks to this short-range wireless technology, you can listen to music using Bluetooth headphones or speakers; you can also type using any Bluetooth keyboard instead of the onscreen keyboard or Apple's optional keyboard dock accessory.

note When shopping for Bluetooth audio products, look for ones that support A2DP (Advanced Audio Distribution Profile). Also, the third-generation iPad supports the Bluetooth 4.0 protocol, a lower-power version that works with devices that maintain long connections (such as some fitness trackers).

Pair the iPad and the device

To communicate with the iPad, a Bluetooth device must be *paired* with it to ensure that the device is recognized and won't get confused by other Bluetooth connections nearby. You need to pair the device only once, after which the iPad identifies and communicates with the keyboard or audio product automatically when it's within range. Follow these steps:

1. Open the Settings app and tap the General category.

2. Tap the Bluetooth option.

3. Ensure that Bluetooth is on; if not, slide the Bluetooth switch to On.

4. Power on the Bluetooth device you want to pair, and put it into its pairing mode; you may need to press and hold a button on the device to switch modes. It will appear in the Devices list (**Figure 1.22**).

Figure 1.22
*Paired and
unpaired devices*

5. If the iPad displays a dialog for pairing, skip to the next step. Otherwise, tap the name of the unpaired device.

6. Enter the device's PIN number.

   For headsets, this is usually "0000" (four zeros), but check the device's instructions if that doesn't work. For keyboards, the PIN is a series of numbers that appears on the iPad screen (**Figure 1.23**).

Figure 1.23
*Pairing the
Apple Wireless
Keyboard*

7. Tap the Connect button. If paired successfully, the device appears as Connected on the Bluetooth screen.

tip The iPad can be paired with more than one device at the same time. For example, you can listen to music through a wireless Bluetooth headset while typing on a Bluetooth keyboard.

tip When you're using a Bluetooth keyboard, the iPad's onscreen keyboard won't appear. This makes sense, except when you're close enough to be in range of the keyboard but not intending to use it. You may need to go into Settings and disable Bluetooth in that case (or turn off the keyboard's power, but is it really worth getting off the couch to do that?).

tip I bought the Apple Wireless Keyboard to use with my iPad, but you can use nearly any Bluetooth keyboard. When you want to turn off the Apple model without disabling Bluetooth on the iPad, press and hold the keyboard's power button for a few seconds until you see the status light disappear.

Forget the Bluetooth device

To remove a device from the list, tap the detail button () and then tap the Forget this Device button.

Mirror Video

On the original iPad, the only way for teachers or presenters to share what was happening on the tablet's screen was to mount a camera above it and project the results. The iPad can mirror its video to an HDTV, digital projector, or other similar device. All you need is an Apple Digital AV Adapter or Apple VGA Adapter; plug it in and mirroring is automatically enabled. Better yet, if you also own an Apple TV, the iPad can mirror its screen over Wi-Fi. Here's how to activate it:

1. Double-press the Home button or swipe up with four fingers to reveal the multitasking bar.

2. Swipe left to right to view the iPad's audio playback, volume, and brightness controls. You should also see an AirPlay button to the right of the fast-forward button.

3. Tap the AirPlay button and choose the Apple TV on your network.

4. Set the Mirroring option to On (**Figure 1.24**).

Figure 1.24
*Start mirroring
the iPad's screen.*

 tip   Here's a related use for your iPad that you may not have considered:
Using Air Display by Avatron Software (www.avatron.com), you can
make the iPad act as a second monitor for your computer. Store chat windows,
Photoshop tools, or anything else—the iPad's screen becomes a spanned extension of your computer's desktop.

Print using AirPrint

It's fun to think we're living in a post-paper world where our news and
books are delivered electronically and we can zap documents across the
world in an instant. But, darn it, sometimes you just need a printed copy
of something. The printing architecture built into the iOS does the job,
although currently Apple supports only a handful of HP printers to which
you can print directly from an iPad.

note   See the following technote at Apple's site for a list of AirPrint-
compatible printers: http://support.apple.com/kb/HT4356.

The act of printing is similar in all apps that support it, whether you're printing a message in Mail or a picture in the Photos app.

1. Tap the Action button (🖅) (**Figure 1.25**). The button may vary depending on the app; in Mail, for example, the Print command is accessible by tapping the Reply button.

Figure 1.25
Find the Print button in the Action menu.

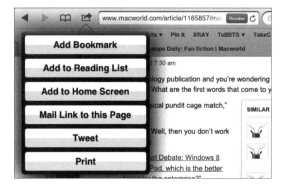

2. In the Printer Options popover, tap the Printer button to choose a connected printer.

3. Choose the number of copies to print. This option may not always be available, depending on which app you're in and which printer you're printing to. Similarly, other options such as double-sided printing depend on the device.

4. Tap the Print button to print the document.

tip Wait, don't give up on printing if you don't have one of the compatible printers! If you own a Mac, download Printopia (www.ecamm.com/mac/printopia/), which enables AirPrint to printers that your computer can access. It also includes the capability to send a file to a Dropbox folder or directly to your Mac. If you run Windows, try the utility AirPrint Activator (www.macerkopf.de/airprint-ios-4-2-1-hack-fuer-windows-user-02481.html).

Search Using Spotlight

Even the smallest-capacity iPad model stores a lot of information. To locate something quickly, go to the Home screen and swipe to the right. (If you're in any Home screen, you can also press the Home button twice; one press takes you to the first Home screen, and the second opens the Spotlight screen. Don't be too quick about the two button presses, though, or you'll open the multitasking bar.)

Type some text into the Search field to bring up results, sorted by apps (**Figure 1.26**). Tap the one you want to jump to. If you don't find what you're looking for, tap the Search Web or Search Wikipedia options to view those search results in Safari.

Figure 1.26
*Spotlight
search results*

iPod music —

Extend search
in Safari

To quickly erase a term and start over, tap the cancel button (⊗) to the right of the Search field.

> **tip** Spotlight also matches app names when you search, so if you have dozens of apps and don't want to navigate to the screen containing the one you want, simply perform a Spotlight search to locate and launch it.

2

Get and Use Apps

The iPad is sleek and shiny, a fantastic example of industrial design that packs a host of cutting-edge technologies into a thin, responsive tablet. Aside from holding it in your hand, however, your time spent using the iPad will be focused almost entirely on its software.

The core apps that ship with the iPad are useful, but those are just the beginning. More than 585,000 (at this writing) programs are available from the App Store, 200,000 of them made specifically for the iPad—so many that Apple's marketing tagline, "There's an app for that," has become part of current popular culture.

With a few taps (and often just a few dollars), you can locate, purchase, and download apps that do nearly anything you can think of. In this chapter, I tell you how to find and install apps, and also how you can share them with friends.

Find and Install Apps

Quick, jump in the car, let's go app shopping!

Or don't. In the case of most software, buying a new program means going to a store in the mall, or buying a box from an online retailer, or even downloading it from the developer directly. But that's not the case with iPad apps.

The only outlet to get apps is Apple's App Store, available on the iPad itself or from within iTunes. Pricing varies among apps, naturally, but most cost less than $15—in many cases, far less, with many apps available for free.

note The App Store does not offer demo or shareware versions of apps, so it's difficult to evaluate an app before purchasing it. It's not impossible, though: Many vendors offer free "light" versions of their apps, which are limited in scope but give you a sense of what the paid version can do. Other apps may cost as little as $0.99 and offer just a handful of features, with the option to unlock others if you pony up some more cash.

The App Store on the iPad

Tap the App Store icon on the Home screen to launch the App Store. Since it's a storefront, you'll see many new and featured titles (**Figure 2.1**). Tap the What's Hot button at the top of the screen to view more featured apps, or tap the Release Date button to see what has been added recently. To view more apps in boxed sections, such as New and Noteworthy, swipe left or right.

tip It's sometimes difficult to get a sense of what an app offers by looking solely at screenshots, so be sure to tap the link that takes you to a developer's Web site for more information. Often companies will include a video of how the app operates.

Figure 2.1

*The App Store
on the iPad*

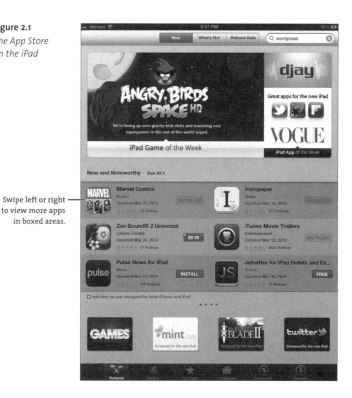

Swipe left or right
to view more apps
in boxed areas.

At the bottom of the screen, the buttons let you view featured apps;
see Genius recommendations of other apps, based on apps you already
own; consult lists of the most popular paid and free apps in Top Charts;
or browse by category. (See "Update Apps," later in this chapter, for more
about the Updates button.) If you already know what you're looking for,
enter its name into the Search field in the upper-right corner of the screen.

To view more information about an app, including screenshots and
customer reviews, tap its icon.

If you decide your life isn't complete without the app, tap the button that displays the price. The button changes to read "Buy App"; if the app is free, you'll see "Install App" (**Figure 2.2**). Tap it again to purchase, or tap anywhere outside the button to switch back to the price.

Figure 2.2
Purchasing an app

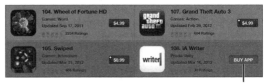

Tap the price to reveal
the Buy App button.

After you enter your iTunes Store account password, the app downloads and is installed in the first open space on the Home screen (**Figure 2.3**).

Figure 2.3
The app appears on the Home screen and is automatically installed.

note If you're connected to the Internet using cellular networking, large apps—over 50 MB—won't be downloaded. Connect to a Wi-Fi network or use iTunes on your computer and try the purchase again. Waiting for Wi-Fi also means you won't chew up your monthly cellular data allotment with app update downloads.

tip The iTunes Store knows which apps you've purchased in the past (for the Apple ID you're signed in with). Those appear with an Install button; no need to re-buy them.

The App Store within iTunes on a computer

It may be more convenient to browse and purchase apps on your computer and then sync them to the iPad later. However, an extra step is required when buying apps in iTunes. Fire up iTunes, click the iTunes Store item in the sidebar, and then click the App Store heading at the top. After clicking the Buy App button, the app is downloaded and added to iTunes. When you next perform a sync, the app is automatically transferred to the iPad and appears on the Home screen.

Automatically install purchased apps

If you already own another iOS device, such as an iPhone, it's likely you want new apps to appear on the iPad as well. Normally you'd have to download a purchased app again on the iPad or sync with iTunes (provided you've synced the iPhone first). Instead, you can opt to automatically download new apps, music, and books.

Go to Settings > Store and turn on the Automatic Downloads option for apps. A similar preference exists in the settings for iTunes, categorized under the Store heading.

Run iPhone apps on the iPad

You'll find apps that are written specifically for the iPad, but your iPad can also run apps written for both the iPhone and iPod touch. In some cases, a single app can run on all three devices—the app contains resources that take advantage of the iPad when run there, but that are ignored when run on an iPhone or iPod touch.

Apps not adapted to the iPad work in one of two ways: either at their actual size centered in the screen, or enlarged to fill the screen. Tap the 2x button in the lower-right corner to scale the app to fill the screen, or tap the 1x button to return to the original size.

Update Apps

When developers update their software, they submit a changed version to the App Store, where Apple approves the update and makes it available. Because everything goes through the App Store, your iPad can check for updates so you don't have to go searching for them online.

A numbered badge appears on the App Store icon in the Home screen indicating how many updates are ready to be downloaded. In iTunes, the badge appears on the Apps item in the sidebar (**Figure 2.4**).

Figure 2.4
*App updates
are available.*

Badge on
App Store icon

Badge in iTunes

note You don't have to wait for the iPad or iTunes to communicate with the Apple mothership. In the App Store app, tap the Updates button to trigger a check for new versions. In iTunes, select the Apps item in the sidebar and then click the Check for Updates button.

To install the updates on the iPad, do the following:

1. Tap the App Store app to launch it.

2. Tap the Updates button in the bottom toolbar. A list of updated apps appears.

3. To learn more about the update, tap its name in the list. Otherwise, skip to the next step.

4. Tap the Free button next to any single app you want to download. When it changes to Install, tap it again.

   Or, tap the Update All button at the top of the screen to download and install all updates at once.

tip A scary-looking dialog may appear before the download begins, warning you that an app may contain material inappropriate for children. Apple is strict about the type of content that's accepted into the App Store, so you shouldn't find anything too suggestive, and certainly nothing explicit. However, Apple can't control all content, especially for apps that fetch data from the Web, so the company throws up this disclaimer.

What if you want to re-download an app you purchased, but you can't remember its exact name? In the App Store app, tap the Purchased button to view your purchase history and download any apps that aren't currently installed on the iPad.

Remove Apps

As you download more apps—and I predict you will—you're going to find that some don't hold the allure they once did, or you'll discover a new app that does something better than the first one you downloaded. You can remove the app on the iPad itself or disable it from syncing within iTunes.

note The original apps that ship with the iPad cannot be removed. If they're in your way, consider moving them to another Home screen (described in "Customize the Home Screen," coming up).

On the iPad

1. Locate the app you want to remove on the Home screen, and then touch and hold its icon for a second. All of the apps begin to shake, and an X button appears on the app's icon.

2. Tap the X button.

3. Tap the Delete button in the confirmation dialog that appears (**Figure 2.5**).

Click here to delete.

Figure 2.5
Remove an app from the iPad.

4. You can optionally rate the app, which will be reflected in its description at the App Store. Tap a star to give a rating from 1 to 5 and then tap the Rate button. Or, tap No Thanks to delete the app without rating it.

In iTunes

1. Connect the iPad to your computer and select its name in the iTunes sidebar.

2. Click the Applications tab in the main section of the screen.

3. Locate the app you wish to remove, either in the list of applications or in the preview area of the different Home screens (**Figure 2.6**).

Figure 2.6
Remove an app in iTunes.

4. Position your mouse pointer over the app you wish to remove and click the X button. Or, in the list, click the checkbox to the left so that it is not marked.

5. Click the Apply button to pass the changes along to the iPad. iTunes asks you to confirm that you want to remove the app, and if you click Yes, the iPad is synced.

Share Apps

Apps you've downloaded can be loaded onto any other iPad, iPhone, or iPod touch that you sync with your computer. But what you may not know is that you can share apps with up to five other computers (including friends' computers) using the Home Sharing feature of iTunes.

For example, let's say I want to play a game of Scrabble for iPad with my wife. I've purchased the app, but she doesn't want to buy a new copy because she may not want to play it often. Here's how to get the app onto another device.

1. Make sure your friend's computer is on the same local network as your computer.

2. Enable Home Sharing in both computers by choosing Advanced > Turn On Home Sharing (if it's not already active).

3. Enter your iTunes account name (the email address you use for purchasing things from the iTunes Store) and password, and then click the Create Home Share button. Be sure to use the same account (yours, since you are sending the app) on both computers.

4. If iTunes asks to authorize the computer, click Yes. On your friend's computer, the name of your iTunes library appears in the sidebar.

5. Choose your library, click the disclosure triangle to the left of the name, and then click the Apps item.

6. Locate the app you want to transfer, and drag it to the Library heading in the sidebar (**Figure 2.7**). The app file copies to your friend's iTunes library. He or she can then sync the iPad to install the app.

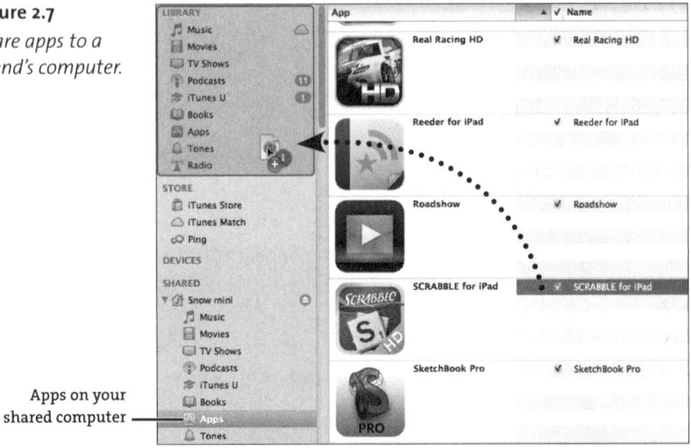

Figure 2.7

Share apps to a friend's computer.

Apps on your shared computer

note Because your friend didn't purchase the app originally, she needs to enter your iTunes password to update the app. If you trust your friend enough to give her your password, that's not a problem, but it also means she can buy anything from the iTunes Store on your dime.

Sharing Apps by Copying Files

The procedure I've just described is the outward-facing approach within iTunes, but you can also share apps by copying their files outside iTunes (if you're comfortable doing that). Here's how:

1. Locate the app you want: In iTunes on a Mac, Control-click the app and choose Show in Finder. Under Windows, right-click the app and choose Show in Windows Explorer.

2. Copy the app file to the other computer over your network (or using a USB memory stick or whatever method you choose).

3. Drag the app file to the iTunes library on the other computer. That installs the app, ready for syncing to the iPad.

Set App Preferences

Every app has its own settings, but finding them can be scattershot. Many apps include preferences within the app itself, so you can do everything in one place. Apple's recommended (and awkward, in my opinion) method is to put preferences within the Settings app (**Figure 2.8**). Scroll to the bottom of the Settings screen to view apps, then tap an app's name to access its preferences.

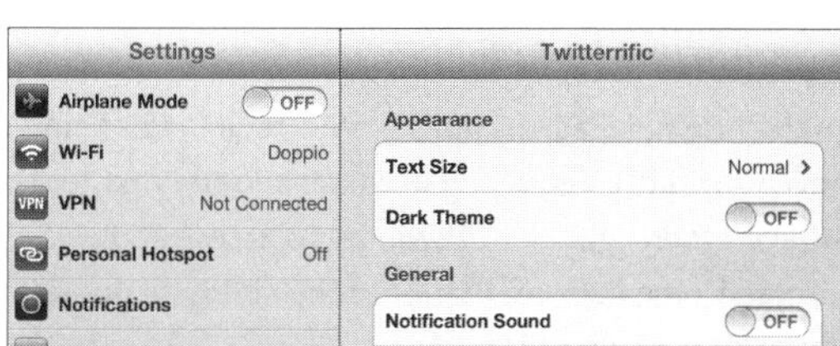

Figure 2.8

App-specific preferences in the Settings app

Customize the Home Screen

I introduced the Home screen in Chapter 1 and mentioned how you can swipe each screenful of apps to find what you're looking for. What I didn't mention was that you can move the apps between screens and organize apps into folders, so you don't have to swipe several times to get a frequently used app that appears on the last screen. It's also possible to change the background image to personalize your iPad.

On the iPad

1. Touch and hold any app for a second until the apps begin to shake.

2. Drag an app you want to move to a different position on the screen. Or, to move an app to another screen, drag it to the left or right edge of the screen and hold it there.

   After a moment, the screen advances and you still have control over positioning the app.

3. Lift your finger to drop the app in place.

4. Press the Home button to return to the Home screen's normal mode.

> **tip** The apps in the Dock at the bottom of each Home screen remain the same, no matter which screen you're viewing. Put your most frequently used apps there.

Organize apps into folders

On the original iPad, my apps were strewn across nine Home screens. I moved my most frequently used apps to the first two or three screens, but even then I got sick of swiping to access apps. Now, my iPad is down to three Home screens, thanks to the ability to put related apps into groups that Apple calls folders.

1. Tap and hold an app you want to move, until all of the app icons are shaking.

2. Drag an app *onto the top* of another app. After a moment, a folder icon appears as a box that contains small thumbnail images of each app, along with an exposed area that displays every app in the folder (**Figure 2.9**).

Figure 2.9
*App added to
a folder group*

3. A name for the folder is automatically assigned based on the categories of the apps, but you can change it. Select the text field and type your own title.

4. Drag other apps onto a folder icon to add them to the folder.

5. Press the Home button to finish rearranging the icons.

When you want to access an app within a folder, tap the folder to expose its contents and then tap the app you wish to open.

tip Maybe you don't want to swipe between Home screens at all. You can just as easily create a folder of apps and then put the folder in the Dock at the bottom of the screen. That approach lets you access 120 apps from the Dock alone, plus 20 more on the first Home screen!

In iTunes

1. Connect the iPad to your computer, select it in the sidebar, and go to the Apps tab.

2. Drag an app to a new location, including to other screens, which are displayed in the right-hand column (**Figure 2.10**). (If the iPad is in its wide orientation, the screen thumbnails appear below the main screen.)

   To create a folder, drag an app onto another app; or drag an app to an existing folder.

   You can also drag an entire Home screen in that column to a different location. This is great if, for example, you keep games on one screen and business apps on another and want to change their order.

    tip **Press Shift and click more than one app in the Apps tab to select several, and then drag them to a new Home screen all at once.**

3. Click the Apply button to sync the changes to the iPad.

Figure 2.10
Drag an app to a new Home screen.

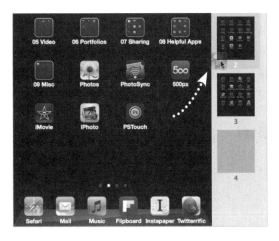

Change the Home screen image

The iPad includes many alternate Home screen images, or you can use one of your own photos as the background. You can also set the image that comes up when you unlock the iPad.

1. Go to Settings > Brightness & Wallpaper.

2. Tap the Wallpaper button, which displays the current Lock and Home screen images.

3. Tap the next Wallpaper button to view images that Apple includes with the iPad. Or, tap the Photo Library button or the name of one of your photo albums to view your images (**Figure 2.11**).

Figure 2.11
Choose an album of wallpaper images.

4. Tap an image to select it and to see a preview of how it will appear.

5. If the image is larger than the iPad's screen resolution (which includes most digital photos), you can refine its appearance. Resize it by using pinch and expand gestures, and reposition it by dragging with one finger.

6. Tap the Set Lock Screen, Set Home Screen, or Set Both button to make the change (**Figure 2.12**). Or, tap Cancel to choose a different image.

Figure 2.12
Set the wallpaper.

3

Browse the Web

Web browsers on smartphones have historically been pretty terrible. The iPhone demonstrated that it's possible to render a Web site that isn't custom programmed to be readable on a mobile device. However, even that didn't prove to be 100 percent accurate, because although Safari on the iPhone *can* render a page as it would appear in a desktop Web browser, the screen size is still a limitation, leading many sites to adjust their code to accommodate.

The iPad, on the other hand, is almost all screen, with a version of Safari that displays Web sites just as you'd see them on a Mac or Windows PC. We no longer wonder or marvel at how we access information online—we just get it.

Access Web Sites

Tap the Safari icon on the Home screen to launch the iPad's Web browser. I'm assuming you have an active Internet connection, either via Wi-Fi or cellular. If not, go back to Chapter 1 for a refresher on getting online.

note As soon as you try to access a Web site in Safari, the program checks for an Internet connection. If one isn't found, the iPad asks if you want to join a nearby Wi-Fi network.

Open and read a new Web page

Safari opens to a new blank page, with a layout similar to what you're accustomed to on your computer.

1. Tap the Address field.

2. Enter the address of the site you want to visit.

To quickly erase what you've typed and start over, tap the cancel button (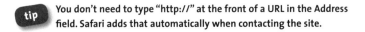) at the right edge of the Address field.

As you type, Safari suggests matching URLs from your bookmarks or history in a popover (**Figure 3.1**).

tip You don't need to type "http://" at the front of a URL in the Address field. Safari adds that automatically when contacting the site.

3. Tap the Go key in the onscreen keypad or a suggested address in the popover. After a few seconds, the page appears.

tip Safari builds its list of suggested sites based on browsing history and bookmarks (see "Create and Organize Bookmarks," later in this chapter).

Figure 3.1
A new Safari window

Back/Next   Bookmarks   Address field   Search field

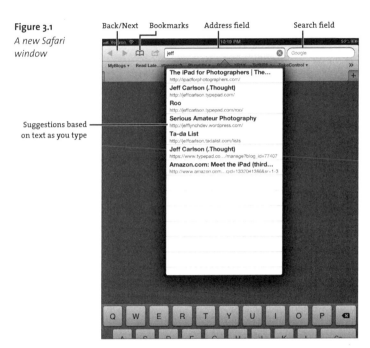

Suggestions based
on text as you type

To read the site's content, flick or drag the page in any direction to scroll it. If you'd like to enlarge an area, double-tap that spot to zoom in—Safari smartly figures out how much zoom to apply based on the page's layout. You can also spread two fingers to enlarge manually. Double-tap or pinch to zoom back out.

 To quickly jump to the top of a Web page, tap the status bar at the top of the screen. (This shortcut works in most apps.)

To follow a link to another page, simply tap the text or image that is linked. You can return to the previous page by tapping the Back button in the toolbar.

Reload or cancel

Tap the icon at the right edge of the address bar (↻) to reload the page. While the content is downloading, the icon becomes a cancel button (✕); tap it if you want to stop loading.

Read uncluttered pages using Reader

Even with the iPad's high-resolution Retina display, text can be small on some Web sites, and sometimes there are so many ads and other distractions that it can be difficult to read an article. Safari's Reader feature can cut through the clutter.

1. Open a Web page that contains an article of some sort. Safari is pretty smart about differentiating between a page with content and a home page with lots of links.

2. Tap the Reader button that appears in the address bar to view the article in a highly readable overlay (**Figure 3.2**).

3. Tap the Text Size button to make the text larger or smaller.

4. When you're done reading, tap the Reader button again.

Figure 3.2
The Reader view

Text Size

View your browsing history

What if you want to view a Web page you loaded yesterday? If you know the site's address, you could start typing it and pick it from the list of possible matches. Or, you could view the entire list of sites you've visited.

1. Tap the Bookmarks button in the toolbar.

2. Choose History in the popover that appears (**Figure 3.3**).

3. Tap the name of the site you visited. You may need to tap a date folder to locate it.

Figure 3.3
Viewing your browsing history

Tapping History shows the folder's contents.

Open new pages

You can browse up to nine pages, which appear as tabs in Safari's interface. To open a new page, do one of the following:

- Tap the New Tab (+) button at the right of the tab bar. An empty Safari window appears, where you can enter a Web address or perform a search. Safari activates the Search field automatically, so if you want to enter a Web address directly, you need to next tap the Address field.

- Another option is to open a link in a new page. Instead of just tapping the link, touch and hold it, and then tap Open in New Tab (**Figure 3.4**).

Figure 3.4
Touch and hold a link to open it in a new tab.

New Tab

tip Bringing up the popover also reveals the link's URL and gives you the option to copy it to the iPad's memory for pasting elsewhere (such as in an outgoing Mail message).

With several pages open at the same time, switch between them by tapping the tab that belongs to the one you want to view.

Close pages

When you no longer wish to keep a Web page open, tap the X button to the left of the title in its tab.

Watch videos

Many videos that appear on Web pages can be viewed within Safari (unless they're delivered using Flash, which the iPad doesn't support). A play button appears on videos you can watch (**Figure 3.5**).

Figure 3.5
Embedded video

Button indicates you can play this video.

Tap the button to begin playing the video. When you do, the iPad's video controls appear (**Figure 3.6**).

Figure 3.6
Playing embedded video

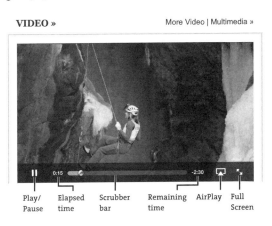

Play/   Elapsed   Scrubber   Remaining   AirPlay   Full
Pause   time   bar   time   Screen

tip   YouTube videos, even those that appear in embedded players on other sites' Web pages, get handed off to the YouTube app for playback.

The scrubber bar displays the video's progress; the light gray portion to the right of the playhead indicates how much of the video has been downloaded. To jump ahead in the movie, drag the playhead across the scrubber bar. The AirPlay button sends the video to an AirPlay-compatible device such as an Apple TV (see Chapter 8 for more on AirPlay). Tap the Full Screen button to enlarge the video to use the entire iPad screen, hiding the rest of the Web page.

> **tip** You can also use a two-fingered expand gesture (moving your fingers apart) on the movie to quickly zoom it into full-screen mode. Once there, double-tap the video to switch between viewing the full width of the movie (with black bars) or filling the screen (which crops the image). See Chapter 8 for more information about playing videos and other media.

Search the Web

What did we do before we could search the Internet for everything? How did we win trivia bets with our friends or recall specific movie quotes (and other important things, I'm sure)? You can navigate to any search engine's Web site, but it's easier to perform the search directly from the toolbar.

Tap the Search field in Safari and start typing your search term (**Figure 3.7**). Tap one of the suggested terms that appear as you type; or, tap the Search key in the onscreen keyboard to go to Google's results page.

Figure 3.7
*Safari's
Search field*

tip Safari uses Google as its default search engine, but you can also choose to set Yahoo or Bing as the source for the Search field. Go to Settings > Safari > Search Engine, and choose Google, Yahoo, or Bing.

Search within a Web page

What good is a search engine if, when you bring up the Web page that contains your search term, it's impossible to find the term? Safari searches within the contents of a Web page, too.

1. With a page loaded, enter your term in the Search field. The first results lead to searches elsewhere on the Web, but the bottom of the list includes an On This Page section (provided there are matches).

2. Tap the Find "[the term]" option. The first instance is highlighted.

3. At the bottom of the screen, tap the Next button to highlight the next instance (**Figure 3.8**).

4. To look for something else on the page, enter the term in the Search field in the lower bar. Or, tap Done to stop searching.

Figure 3.8
Searching within the page

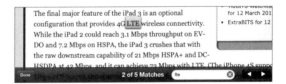

note You're not limited to using Safari's default Search field. In addition to going to any search engine's Web site, several standalone search apps are available, such as Microsoft's Bing and, yes, even Google. They typically add other features not available in a Web browser; for example, you can speak a search term to the Google app, which deciphers what you said and delivers its results.

Read Pages Later with Reading List

In an ideal world, I'd sit all day and read the dozens of interesting articles and Web sites that I run across on Twitter, Facebook, email, and other outlets. Instead, I live in the real world, but I can offload a lot of that reading until it's more convenient by using Safari's Reading List. It remembers the link of a Web page so you can load the page later. To add a page to Reading List, do the following:

1. With a page loaded that you want to read later, tap the Action button to the left of the Address field.

2. Tap the Add to Reading List button. The page location is saved and automatically shared to your other devices via iCloud.

When you're ready to read the page on the iPad, tap the Bookmarks button and choose Reading List. You can list everything you've saved or just pages you haven't read (**Figure 3.9**). Tap a page to load it.

Figure 3.9
An item added to Reading List

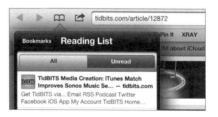

tip To delete an item from Reading List, swipe left to right and then tap the Delete button.

tip If Reading List sounds like a glorified bookmark, well, it is. You still require an Internet connection to load the pages later. I prefer to save articles to Instapaper, which stores the text—not ads or layout—for online or offline reading. See the sidebar "Expand Safari's Capabilities with Bookmarklets," later in this chapter.

Create and Organize Bookmarks

A Web browser is a great reference tool, not just because there are more than 1 trillion Web pages on the Internet (Google's estimate in 2008), but because you can store bookmarks for sites that you want to visit later. Safari on the iPad can create bookmarks and also use the bookmarks you've created on your computer.

Open a bookmarked page

Apple includes a few basic bookmarks in Safari, which will give us a sense of how opening a bookmark works. Tap the Bookmarks button on the toolbar, and then tap the name of a Web page from the list to load it.

 tip Here's a handy bookmark: Apple includes a Web version of the iPad User Guide at the bottom of the Bookmarks list.

Create a new bookmark

When you find a page you want to return to later, do the following:

1. Tap the Action button in the toolbar.

2. In the popover that appears, tap the Add Bookmark button.

3. Edit the name of the bookmark, if you wish (**Figure 3.10**).

Figure 3.10
*Create a
bookmark.*

4. Tap the button at the bottom of the popover and choose where the bookmark will be located in the Bookmarks hierarchy.

   Typically, there are just two levels to the hierarchy: the Bookmarks folder itself and the Bookmarks Bar, a subfolder whose contents appear as clickable shortcuts beneath the toolbar. (It's also possible to import the bookmarks from your computer, via iTunes or iCloud.)

5. Tap the Save button to create the bookmark.

> **tip** I store nearly all of my active bookmarks on the Bookmarks Bar, organized in Safari on my Mac. For that reason, I choose to make the Bookmarks Bar always visible in Safari (normally it appears only when you're typing in the Address or Search field). To do this, go to Settings > Safari and enable the Always Show Bookmarks Bar option.

Edit a bookmark

Suppose you realize that your bookmark's name is too long to fit with other bookmarks on the Bookmarks Bar, or you want to put it into a different subfolder. Here's how to edit existing bookmarks on the iPad.

1. Tap the Bookmarks button on the toolbar.

2. Locate the bookmark you want to edit; this could mean tapping a subfolder (like Bookmarks Bar) to view its contents.

3. Tap the Edit button in the popover's navigation bar. The items in the list gain red icons to the left of their names (**Figure 3.11**).

4. Edit the bookmark in any of the following ways:

   ▪ To reposition the item within the list, touch the icon at the far right and drag it to a new position.

Figure 3.11
*Editing the
Bookmarks list*

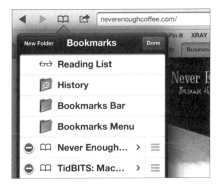

- Tap the bookmark name to change the title or URL. This is also where you can move the bookmark to another subfolder by tapping the button at the bottom of the popover. Use the navigation button at the top of the popover to return to the enclosing folder, or simply tap anywhere outside it to apply the change.

- To remove a bookmark, tap the red icon to the left of its name, which displays a Delete button to the right. Tap that Delete button to remove the bookmark. (This two-step process is designed to avoid accidentally deleting bookmarks.)

5. Tap the Done button to exit the editing mode.

 tip   A faster method of deleting bookmarks is to swipe left-to-right across the item's name to bring up the Delete button.

note   I use iCloud to synchronize my Safari bookmarks between my computer and all of my devices. iTunes can also synchronize bookmarks with the Mac or Windows version of Safari and with Internet Explorer 8 or later under Windows. See Chapter 10 for more information on syncing.

tip The app Handoff (www.handoffapp.com) does something cool: If you're viewing a Web page on your computer, send it to your iPad using a button that appears in the browser's toolbar. When you launch Handoff on the iPad, the page can be loaded, read within the Handoff app, or opened in Safari.

Add a Web page to the Home screen

What if you want to jump to a frequently viewed Web page more quickly than navigating bookmarks? Create a Home screen icon for it.

1. In Safari, navigate to the page you want to bookmark.

2. Tap the Action button.

3. Tap the Add to Home Screen button.

4. In the popover that appears, edit the icon's name (**Figure 3.12**).

5. Tap the Add button. The new icon appears on the Home screen.

   Tapping that icon opens the Web page in a new Safari window.

Figure 3.12
*Creating a
Home screen icon*

Editing the name

Icon on
Home screen

Share a page's address via email

You can easily share a Web page with someone by sending them a link via email. Tap the Action button and choose Mail Link to this Page from the popover. A new outgoing email address appears with the page title already entered into the Subject field and the link in the body. All you have to do is enter a recipient's email address and tap Send.

Share a page via Twitter

Twitter, if you're not already aware, is a service that lets you publish short snippets—140 characters or less—on the Internet, readable by anyone who follows your Twitter account or accesses your Twitter page on the Web. Apple supports Twitter at the system level, making it easy to share information to your Twitter followers without requiring a dedicated app. (Set up your Twitter account information in Settings > Twitter.)

In this case, if you run across a Web page you think others would like, you can share its address directly from within Safari.

1. Tap the Action button and choose Tweet from the list of options.

2. In the Tweet dialog that appears, enter text that will accompany the Web address (**Figure 3.13**). Optionally, tap the Add Location button if you want to share your current physical location.

3. Tap Send to post the tweet to your account.

Figure 3.13
Sharing a Web page via Twitter

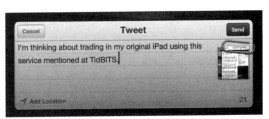

Expand Safari's Capabilities with Bookmarklets

Safari supports JavaScript, a scripting language that offers all sorts of interactivity on the Web, including bookmarklets—tiny bookmarks that use JavaScript code instead of a Web site address. What does that mean for non-developers? It adds features that Safari lacks.

For example, one of my favorite iPad and iPhone apps is Instapaper (www.instapaper.com). When I'm viewing a Web page that I want to read later—a long article, for example—I tap a "Read Later" bookmarklet that Instapaper created in my Bookmarks Bar, which adds the page to my Instapaper account. Later, in Instapaper, I can read the page without being online, and in a format that strips out all the junk surrounding most Web pages (**Figure 3.14**). (Many third-party apps include Instapaper support natively, avoiding the need to take a side trip to Safari and activate a bookmarklet.)

Figure 3.14

The same article in Safari and Instapaper

Safari

Instapaper

To find more, search for "bookmarklet" in your favorite search engine and explore.

AutoFill Forms

How many Web sites do you visit that require some sort of account? There's no way I can keep track of all the logins and passwords for various news, travel, and shopping sites. One option is to simply use the same password for everything, but that's dangerous. If someone were to discover that password, they'd have access to all of your sites.

Safari's AutoFill feature can keep track of those credentials for you and give you the option of filling in the information with one tap.

tip While we're talking about security, allow me to recommend 1Password (www.agilebits.com), a great secure repository for all of your logins and other sensitive information. 1Password exists as an application for the Mac or Windows, and as an app for the iPad/iPhone/iPod touch. On my Mac it's essential, letting me easily fill in logins and storing new logins as I create them. It can also keep my credit card information handy for when I'm making purchases. The mobile app can't tie directly into Safari (due to restrictions imposed by Apple on sharing data between apps), but it's very handy when I need to look up a login. The best part: if you have both the iOS app and the desktop version, you can sync your logins between the computer and the device.

Enable AutoFill

Before we start capturing passwords, we need to make sure AutoFill is turned on.

1. Go to Settings > Safari > AutoFill.

2. Toggle the switch for Names and Passwords to On.

3. If you want Safari to fill in personal information such as your name and address in forms, to save you from typing it all, enable the Use Contact Info option. Tap My Info to locate the entry for yourself in the Contacts app (see Chapter 10 for more information).

Store a new login

The first time you fill out a form, you have the option to save it.

1. When you tap a form field, the onscreen keyboard appears with buttons for jumping to the Previous or Next field (which is often easier than moving your fingers from the keyboard and tapping the next or previous field on the page) and for using AutoFill (**Figure 3.15**).

Figure 3.15
Filling in a form

Form buttons

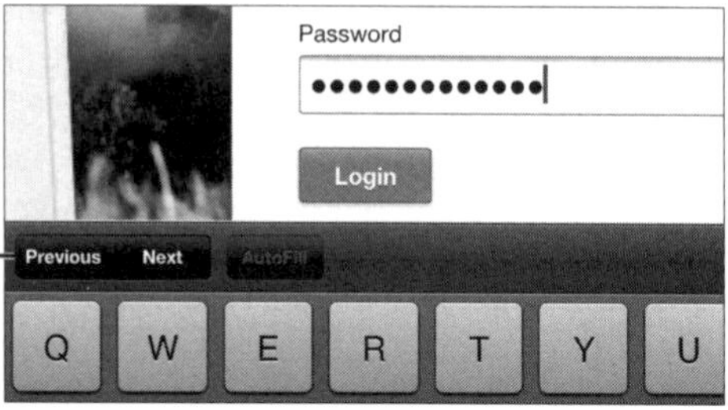

2. Type the relevant information in the fields.

3. Tap the Go button in the onscreen keyboard, or tap the button that submits the data on the Web page (which may be labeled Submit, Log In, Go, or any number of other terse verbs).

4. In the dialog that appears, choose one of the following:

   - **Yes:** Save the password for later. The next time you visit, the name and password will automatically be filled in.

   - **Never for this Website:** Do not save the password, and never ask about saving it for this site in the future. I use this option when accessing sensitive sites such as my bank, where I'd prefer to manually enter the password each time.

   - **Not Now:** Ignore AutoFill for now, but allow Safari to ask you about it next time.

AutoFill contact information

When you encounter a form that asks for your personal information, tap one of the fields to bring up the keyboard and then tap the AutoFill button. The data from your Contacts entry appears (**Figure 3.16**).

Figure 3.16
Using AutoFill for contact information

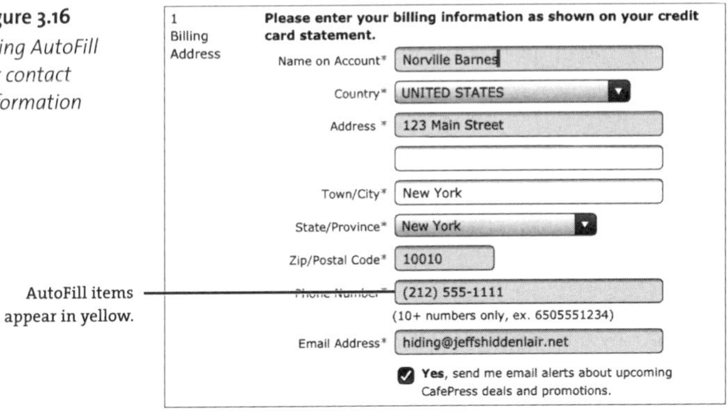

AutoFill items appear in yellow.

1 Billing Address	Please enter your billing information as shown on your credit card statement.
	Name on Account*	Norville Barnes
	Country*	UNITED STATES
	Address *	123 Main Street
	Town/City*	New York
	State/Province*	New York
	Zip/Postal Code*	10010
	Phone Number	(212) 555-1111
		(10+ numbers only, ex. 6505551234)
	Email Address*	hiding@jeffshiddenlair.net
		☑ **Yes**, send me email alerts about upcoming CafePress deals and promotions.

Maintain Web Privacy

Safari's settings contain several options that are designed to limit how your data is used. Go to Settings > Safari and enable or disable the following options:

- **Private Browsing:** Enable this option to prevent Safari from storing your browsing history and revealing any other personal information.

- **Accept Cookies:** By default, Safari only stores cookies—small bits of code that save some preferences or track your visit—created by sites you visit. You can also Never accept cookies or Always accept them.

- **Clear History:** Tap this button to erase your entire browsing history.

The Clear History feature is also available as a button in the navigation bar when you're viewing the History folder from the Bookmarks list.

- **Clear Cookies and Data:** In addition to cookies, Safari stores the contents of recent Web pages so that if you return to a site, it doesn't need to re-download images and other data that may not have changed. If you see a Web page that doesn't seem to have changed its content, try tapping this option to clear Safari's data cache and force a reload.

- **Fraud Warning:** If you follow a link to a site that's known to be a security risk, Safari gives you a warning and the option to continue.

- **JavaScript:** If you're concerned that a site may be using JavaScript to do something nefarious (like masquerade as a legitimate site), you can turn JavaScript off.

- **Block Pop-ups:** Prevent sites from automatically loading new browser windows, which are usually annoying ads.

 The Clear buttons erase all stored data; you can't go in and delete individual cookies, as is possible in most desktop Web browsers.

4

Communicate Using Mail and Messages

Email is a prime candidate for liberation from the desktop. A lot of what I do occurs via email, whether I'm corresponding with friends and relatives or tossing around ideas for upcoming projects. But there's no reason all of that has to happen in front of a computer.

Using the Mail app on the iPad, you can quickly read and reply to messages and dash off notes you may have otherwise ignored because of the hassle of doing it on the computer. Mail also handles incoming file attachments, making it a gateway for sending and receiving files.

Sometimes, though, even email is overkill or too slow when you want to just send a quick note to someone. The Messages app brings instant messaging—a feature usually found on cell phones—to the iPad. And as long as the recipient also has a device running Messages, the texts you send are free (not charged the exorbitant rates of SMS messages).

Set Up Mail

Most likely, you already have email accounts set up on the computer you use to sync with the iPad. You can also set up an account on the iPad itself—for example, you may want to use an iCloud account on the iPad for personal mail that isn't synced to a work computer.

Sync mail accounts from a computer

Mail accounts you've set up in Mail on the Mac, or in Outlook 2010, Outlook 2007, Outlook 2003, or Outlook Express under Windows, appear in iTunes.

1. With the iPad connected to your computer, select its name in the sidebar and then click the Info tab (**Figure 4.1**).

Figure 4.1
*Mail accounts
listed in iTunes*

2. Click the checkbox for Sync Mail Accounts, and then enable accounts you wish to access on the iPad.

3. Click the Sync button. The accounts' settings are added to the iPad's Mail app. Syncing transfers only the account settings, not any of the messages on your computer.

Set up an account on the iPad

If an account isn't set up on the computer you sync to, it's easy to add it directly on the iPad. Mail can automatically configure accounts from iCloud, Gmail, Yahoo Mail, and AOL, as well as Microsoft Exchange accounts, provided you have your account name and password.

note The options on the iPad apply only to email accounts you've previously created. If you want to sign up for a new service—say, a new Gmail account—you need to do that on your computer or using Safari on the iPad.

1. Go to Settings > Mail, Contacts, Calendars.

2. Under the Accounts heading, tap the Add Account button.

3. Tap a service name that matches your account.

   If you get your email from a different provider, tap the Other button and then tap the Add Mail Account button.

4. Enter a name for the account, the email address, and the password (**Figure 4.2**). The Description field automatically fills in the name of the service, but you can edit it separately if you prefer.

Figure 4.2
Enter account information.

5. Tap the Next button. The system verifies the information.

   If you're setting up an Other account, enter the account type (IMAP or POP) and the incoming and outgoing mail server information that your provider gave you when you signed up.

6. For services that support it, you can also set up over-the-air syncing of contacts, calendars, and bookmarks. Make any of those services available by tapping their On buttons in the next screen. (See Chapter 10 for more on syncing personal information.)

7. Tap the Save button to finish setting up the account.

tip If you're setting up an iCloud account, this is a good opportunity to enable the Find My iPad feature, which can locate the iPad on a map if you think it's lost or stolen. See Chapter 11 for more detail.

tip If you're still having trouble configuring an account, check out this form from Apple to help you get the right information from your service provider: http://support.apple.com/kb/HT1277.

Read Mail Messages

Before the iPad, I thought the iPhone's implementation of Mail was fine. Not great, but after all, email is mostly just text, right? Now that I've used Mail on the iPad, though, the iPhone version seems like I'm viewing my messages through a keyhole. It works, but the added screen real estate of the iPad makes a huge difference.

Mail presents two different views of your messages, depending on whether you're viewing the iPad in landscape or portrait orientation. The widescreen view displays mailboxes in a pane at left, with the currently selected message at right (**Figure 4.3**). Tap a message to view it.

Figure 4.3
Mail in landscape orientation

Active message ——

Unread message ——

The tall view displays only the current message. To browse messages one by one, tap the Previous and Next buttons (**Figure 4.4**). Or, to view and access other messages in the mailbox, tap the button at upper left, which is labeled with the name of the active mailbox. The list of messages slides into view.

Figure 4.4
*Mail in portrait
orientation*

Tap to view messages in mailbox.

Previous/Next
message

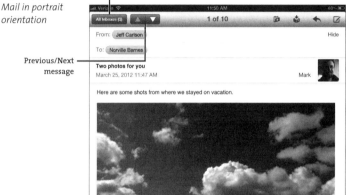

Here are some shots from where we stayed on vacation.

tip Instead of tapping the mailbox name to view the messages list, swipe anywhere using one finger left to right. I use this shortcut all the time.

tip While reading a message, easily enlarge the body text by spreading two fingers in the pinch-outward gesture.

tip Tap the Details link in the upper-right corner of a message to reveal the To and Cc fields, which are otherwise hidden. (You can also make sure they're visible by default; go to Settings > Mail, Contacts, Calendars and set the Show To/Cc Label switch to On.) Showing details also presents the Mark as Unread option, which I often tap after reading an important message to make sure I see the email later when I'm catching up on my computer.

Read email conversations

Email is a time-delayed medium: You could send a message to a friend, who replies several hours later, and then you respond to his message a few minutes after that. Meanwhile, other messages are arriving in your Inbox. Mail helps you keep conversations sensible by grouping them.

Look for a number and angle-bracket (>) symbol to the right of a message's preview; the number indicates how many messages are in the conversation (**Figure 4.5**). Tap that message to reveal a list of the messages in that conversation.

Figure 4.5
Viewing an email conversation

A conversation containing four messages

Mailbox   Messages in the conversation

Navigate accounts and mailboxes

It's not unusual for someone to have more than one email account. Mail's unified Inbox displays all incoming messages as if they're in one mailbox. The unified Inbox is the default view, as you can see in the figure above; the title of the message list indicates you're viewing "All Inboxes," with a number indicating how many messages are unread.

When you do want to dig into specific mailboxes, you can use the controls in the navigation bar that appears either at the top of the left-hand pane (landscape orientation) or at the top of the list slider (portrait orientation). This works for accessing any account's mailboxes, such as Sent Mail, not just the Inbox.

1. Tap the Mailboxes button to view the Mailboxes and Accounts lists (**Figure 4.6**).

2. Tap the name of an account.

3. Tap a mailbox to open it.

4. Tap the message you want to read.

Figure 4.6
Navigating an account hierarchy

Tap Mailboxes button.   Tap mailbox.   Tap message.

tip To preview more of each message in the mailbox list, go to Settings > Mail, Contacts, Calendars; tap the Preview button; and choose up to five visible lines of text.

tip Although you may have hundreds (or thousands!) of messages in a mailbox, Mail keeps the list trim by showing only the 50 most recent items. To view up to 200 messages, go to Settings > Mail, Contacts, Calendars and tap the Show button. You're given the choice of viewing 50, 100, 200, 500, or 1000 recent messages in any given account.

View file attachments

Although email isn't the most effective delivery mechanism for sending files, people frequently attach documents to messages. Mail on the iPad does a good job of handling most common types of files you're likely to encounter, such as images, PDF files, and Microsoft Word documents, among others.

A file attachment is included in the body of a message (**Figure 4.7**). The appearance of the attachment depends on the file's type and size:

- Images generally appear unaltered, as long as Mail can preview the format.

- Large files are not automatically downloaded, and appear with a dotted outline and generic download icon.

- A file that Mail cannot display within the message body shows up as an icon containing the file name and size.

Figure 4.7
File attachments

Microsoft Word file

To preview or open an attachment, do the following:

1. Tap the icon to see a full-screen preview (if Mail can read it), which Apple calls Quick Look.

2. In the preview, tap the Action button in the upper-right corner of the screen. A popover lists which apps can work with the file; tap one to launch the app and open the file. You can also print the attachment from here.

tip If a compatible app is installed, the file attachment icon reflects that app's document format, so it's usually easy to tell right away whether you can open an attachment.

You can also access those options directly without first viewing the Quick Look preview. Touch and hold the icon until a popover appears with options to open in a compatible app or to choose another (**Figure 4.8**).

Figure 4.8
Choose how to view or open the attachment.

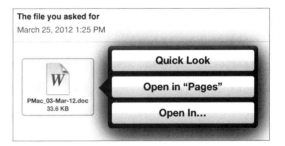

The file you asked for
March 25, 2012 1:25 PM

PMac_03-Mar-12.doc
33.6 KB

Quick Look

Open in "Pages"

Open In...

Act on special data

As you read your email, Mail recognizes some data types and turns them into links. Tapping a Web address, as you might expect, opens the site in Safari. But Mail can also identify and act on street addresses, phone numbers, and email addresses. Tap an email address, and a new outgoing message is created. Tap a street address, and the Maps app launches and shows you the location.

You can also choose how to interact with the data. Touch and hold a link and then choose an option from the popover that appears (**Figure 4.9**).

Figure 4.9
*Acting on a link
in a message*

The Copy
option grabs the
entire address.

View information about senders and recipients

In its attempt to shield people from complexity, Apple chose to show email senders and recipients as friendly named blobs instead of addresses like "norville.barnes.hud@gmail.com." Those blobs become useful buttons, however.

Tap any sender or recipient to view more information. If the person is not in your list of contacts, you can easily add them by tapping the Create New Contact button (**Figure 4.10**). The popover changes to let you edit contact information; tap Done to add the person to your Contacts list. Or, tap Add to Existing Contact if this is a different address for someone you already know.

On the other hand, tapping the button of a person already in your address book displays all of their information. That makes it easy to tap their address to view the location in the Maps app, for example.

Figure 4.10
Viewing sender information

Add the sender to
your Contacts list, or
add the address to
an existing contact.

A new sender   Someone you already know

tip   Viewing information about a sender or recipient also reveals a neat
shortcut. Say you want to send a friend the contact information of
someone else you know. Instead of opening the Contacts app, you can do it
from within Mail. Locate a message from—or addressed to—the person whose
information you want to share. Tap the person's name. In the popover that
appears, scroll to the bottom of the information and tap the Share Contact
button. A new outgoing message is created with the contact's information
stored in a vCard (.vcf) file as an attachment. When your friend receives the
email, he can add the vCard file to his contact-management software.

Check for new mail

When the iPad is connected to the Internet, it can check for new
messages, even when Mail isn't the active app, using two methods: Push,
where new messages are delivered to Mail as soon as they're available;
and Fetch, where Mail contacts each account's server to see if there are
any new messages. Of course, you can also perform a manual check
whenever you want.

Check mail manually

Opening the Mail app triggers a check for new messages, so that's usually all you need to do. If you're eagerly awaiting a response from someone, you can also tap the Refresh button (🔄) at the bottom of the side panel or popover to load new mail.

Get new mail using Push

Push is available for iCloud, Exchange, and Yahoo accounts. Do the following to enable it:

1. Go to Settings > Mail, Contacts, Calendars.

2. Tap the Fetch New Data button.

3. Make sure the Push option is set to On.

Generally, Push applies to all of your accounts that support the feature. However, it's possible to disable Push for some accounts: On the same Fetch New Data screen as above, tap the Advanced button, tap an account name, and then choose the Fetch or Manual option instead of Push.

Check mail on a schedule

For accounts that can't use Push, you can specify an interval for when Mail does its check, which happens in the background no matter which app is running and even if the iPad is asleep.

1. Go to Settings > Mail, Contacts, Calendars.

2. Tap the Fetch New Data button.

3. Tap a time interval to select it (**Figure 4.11**). If you choose Manually, the accounts are checked only when you open Mail or tap the Refresh button.

Figure 4.11
Specify how often Mail checks for new messages.

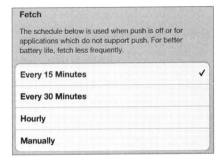

Fetch

The schedule below is used when push is off or for applications which do not support push. For better battery life, fetch less frequently.

Every 15 Minutes	✓
Every 30 Minutes	
Hourly	
Manually	

> **note** Since the iPad is a mobile device, it's likely you could be checking mail using a cellular network connection or on a Wi-Fi network that doesn't belong to you, like at a coffee shop. If you're concerned about securing the Internet connection, see Chapter 11 to learn how to set up a VPN (virtual private network).

When new mail arrives, the Mail icon on the Home screen appears with a badge indicating the total number of unread messages in all accounts. The mailbox navigation button within Mail also displays an unread message count (**Figure 4.12**).

Figure 4.12
New mail indicators

Number of unread messages

Compose Mail Messages

If only we could sit back in lounge chairs, feet propped on a table, and read email all day long like the people in Apple's iPad commercials. Alas, email demands interaction, so at some point you'll find yourself writing new messages and replying to existing ones.

Create a new message

In Mail, do the following:

1. Tap the New Message button (□). An empty message appears.

2. In the To field, begin typing the name of the person you want to send the email to. Mail displays a list of possible contacts (**Figure 4.13**); tap one to enter it.

   You can also tap the Add (⊕) button to view a popover containing all your contacts; scroll or use the Search field to locate a person.

Figure 4.13
List of suggested mail recipients

> **tip** You can type any part of a person's name or email address to find a match; you don't need to always begin with the correct address or the person's first name.

3. If you want to copy other people on the message, tap the Cc/Bcc, From field. Enter addresses into the Cc (carbon copy) or Bcc (blind carbon copy) fields.

If you prefer to send the message from another account, tap the From field and choose one from the popover that appears.

tip Mail's preferences include an option to specify a default outgoing account (go to Settings > Mail, Contacts, Calendars; tap the Default Account button; and select one of your accounts). However, the setting applies only when you're creating new messages in other apps, such as when you send a link to a Web page in Safari. When you create a new message in Mail, the message is addressed as coming from whichever account you're currently viewing.

4. Tap the Subject field and enter a short title. (Don't leave it blank; many mail servers flag messages with empty Subject lines as spam.)

5. Type or dictate your message into the main field (**Figure 4.14**).

Figure 4.14
Writing the email message

6. When you're finished, tap the Send button.

If you're not ready to dispatch the message, tap the Cancel button and then tap Save to store the email in the Drafts folder for editing and sending later.

note Outgoing messages have the text "Sent from my iPad" appended to the end, a bit of text called a signature. You can change the text in Mail's preferences. Go to Settings > Mail, Contacts, Calendars and tap the Signature button. Edit the text to whatever you like, then apply the change by returning to the Mail, Contacts, Calendars screen.

tip Mail's messages can handle more than just text, as I mentioned when talking about opening file attachments earlier. For outgoing messages, for example, this means you could copy a block of content on a Web page in Safari—with its text formatting and graphics—and paste it into a Mail message.

Reply to a message or forward it

When a message requires a response, reply to the sender:

1. With a message open, tap the Reply/Forward button (↩).

2. Tap Reply in the popover that appears. A new outgoing message is created, with the contents of the previous message quoted at the bottom of the message area.

3. Type your reply and then tap Send.

tip When you reply to or forward a message, the entire referenced message is quoted. Often it's better to include just one relevant line or paragraph that you're responding to. Before tapping the Reply/Forward button, select the range of text to quote; only that section appears (Figure 4.15).

Figure 4.15
Replying with selected text

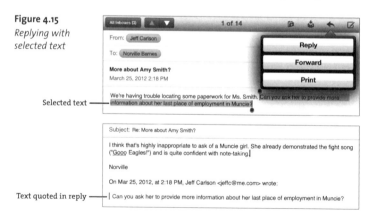

Selected text ——

Text quoted in reply ——

note There's no way to attach a file in an outgoing message within Mail. That doesn't mean attachments aren't possible, though. You just need to do it from whichever app has the content you wish to share via email. For example, in the Photos app you can share a photo by email, which creates a new outgoing mail message with the photo already attached.

Manage Mail Messages

It doesn't take long before email starts to pile up, and even though it's not the same as a foot-high stack of paper letters, I find confronting an Inbox with hundreds of messages a psychic drain. Mail on the iPad doesn't have the same depth of features for managing email that you'll find in a desktop application, but it does let you delete, file, and search for messages.

Delete a message

Unless you're an obsessive archivist, don't try to keep every message. To delete a message after you've read it, tap the Delete (🗑) button in the toolbar. (For some accounts, like Gmail, the Delete button is replaced by an Archive [📥] button.) The message is moved to the account's Trash folder.

Even better, delete a message without reading it. When you're viewing the contents of a mailbox and see a message that's clearly undesirable (I get a lot of spam, can you tell?), do this: swipe one finger across the item from the left or the right. Then tap the Delete button (**Figure 4.16**).

Figure 4.16
Swipe to delete.

Swipe across. ———

——— Tap to delete.

Dealing with Email Spam

Unfortunately, the Mail app doesn't offer any help with unsolicited junk mail, making the iPad less desirable as one's primary destination for email. However, you don't need to be an IT administrator to cut down the amount of spam that reaches your Inbox. Most Internet service providers offer spam filtering at the server level, so a lot of the dreck out there gets trapped before it reaches your iPad.

Move a message

To keep a message but get it out of the way in your Inbox, file it in another folder within your account.

1. With the message open, tap the Move button (📁).

2. Tap a mailbox in the Mailboxes list in the sidebar to move the message there (**Figure 4.17**).

Figure 4.17
*Moving a
message*

Delete or move multiple messages

Sending messages to the Trash or to other mailboxes one by one will make you crazy if there are many to process. Instead, delete or move them in batches.

1. Display the contents of a mailbox, either by tapping its name in the toolbar in portrait orientation or by turning to landscape orientation.

2. Tap the Edit button in the navigation bar.

3. Tap the messages you wish to delete or move. The ones you select gain a red checkmark and appear in a stack to the right (**Figure 4.18**).

Figure 4.18
Process multiple
messages.

Selected messages —

Delete, Move, and
Mark buttons —

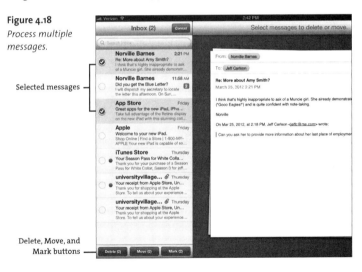

4. Tap the Delete, Move, or Mark button at the lower-left corner of the mailbox. (The Mark button can set the message status as Unread or Flagged, for your attention later.) Or, tap the Cancel button at the top if you change your mind.

Search for messages

A powerful tool in managing piles of email is the capability to find something quickly by performing a search. In this respect, Mail provides some help, though I'm hoping for more in the future.

1. Go to the mailbox you want to search and then tap the Search field.

2. Tap a button to specify which portion of the messages should be searched: the From field, the To field, the Subject field, or All.

note That's right, there's (still!) no option to search the *contents* of your messages, which boggles my mind. I continue to hope the capability arrives in a future version of iOS.

3. Type a term in the Search field. Results appear in the list (**Figure 4.19**).

4. Tap a message to read it.

Figure 4.19
Searching a mailbox

Mail initially looks through the messages that have been downloaded to the iPad. If you don't find what you're looking for, tap the Continue Search on Server option at the bottom of the list to query the mail server for more results.

tip   Another limitation of Mail's built-in search is that you can only peer
into either all Inboxes or one active mailbox at a time. There's a better
way, however. Go to the Home screen and perform a Spotlight search instead
(Figure 4.20). You'll get results from every searchable app, but it's easy enough
to scroll down to the Mail messages, which are pulled from all mailboxes.

Figure 4.20
*Search results
using Spotlight*

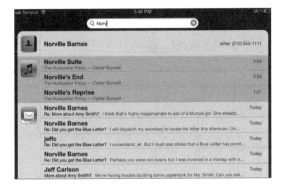

Communicate Using Messages

Cell phone owners have long enjoyed (and abused in quantity) the ability to send and receive SMS texts, which turn out to be enormously
expensive relative to the amount of data that's actually being sent. With
its Messages app, Apple broke the cellular carriers' chokehold on texts
by sending the same data over the Internet for free. The iPad isn't a cell
phone, but using the Messages app, you can communicate with other
people who own a device running iOS 5.0 or later.

Set up Messages

Instead of identifying you using a cell phone number, Messages uses your
email address to route incoming messages from others. Messages uses

your Apple ID by default. However, you can also specify other addresses that people can use to send messages to you.

1. Go to Settings > Messages and tap the Receive At button.

2. Tap Add Another Email and enter an email address.

3. Go back to the Messages screen to apply the setting.

Send a text message

You can send a text to an email address or a phone number (provided the number belongs to someone who also has Messages on their iPhone).

1. In Messages, tap the New Message button ( ).

2. Type the name or address of the person to whom you want to communicate in the To field that appears.

3. In the message line just above the keyboard, type or dictate a message (**Figure 4.21**). It's also possible to send photos or videos—tap the camera button to capture a new shot or choose from your photo library.

4. Tap Send.

Conversations appear above the message line in dialog balloons.

Figure 4.21
Sending a text in Messages

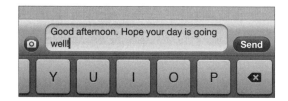

> **tip** Touch and hold a dialog balloon to bring up the option to copy its contents, if you want to paste it elsewhere (such as Mail).

5

Capture Photos and Video

The iPad includes two built-in cameras for capturing photos and video: one mounted on the back and one at the front. The front-facing one isn't great—it's the same camera introduced in the iPad 2—but it's fine for FaceTime video calls. The camera on the back, however, is a nice upgrade if you had the displeasure of using the one in the iPad 2. (I'm being harsh, but that camera's resolution and quality wasn't up to the level I expect from Apple.) The rear camera on the third-generation iPad captures 5 megapixels of data, features great lens elements, and captures 1080p video with automatic image stabilization.

And yet, specifications quickly lose their importance when you're video-chatting with a friend in another city or capturing a photo or video that you otherwise might have missed. Specs improve over time, but events happen now.

Shoot Photos

Many apps take advantage of the cameras—if you haven't already played with the included Photo Booth app (**Figure 5.1**), definitely check it out for a lot of fun—but I'll cover the basics of using the iPad's Camera app.

Figure 5.1
The many faces of Photo Booth

Capture a photo

You know how camera manufacturers boast that their cameras have large 2.5-inch or 3-inch LCD screens? How about a 9.7-inch screen? When you open the Camera app, nearly the entire screen is a preview of what you're about to capture. Here are the basics of getting a shot; I'll go into some of the options shortly.

1. Tap the Camera app to open it.

2. Compose your shot using the preview on the screen (**Figure 5.2**); you can hold the iPad in portrait or landscape orientation and it senses the difference.

To toggle between the rear and front cameras, tap the Camera Switch button.

If you see one or more green boxes appear, the Camera app is identifying what it thinks is a person's face. When you take the shot, it uses that area as the focus point.

Figure 5.2
The Camera app interface

                                    Shutter button   Switch cameras

3. Press the shutter button to take a shot.

The photo is saved in the iPad's Camera Roll, which is accessible by tapping the preview button in the lower-left corner of the screen or by opening the Photos app. (See Chapter 6 for more on viewing photos.)

 Tapping the shutter button can sometimes result in a blurry photo due to the vibration from making the tap. If you're seeing excessively fuzzy pictures, try this: Touch and hold the shutter button. Then, line up your shot and release the button when you're ready to capture the photo.

 To help you line up the photo, tap the Options button and enable the onscreen grid.

Choose a focus point, exposure, and white balance

The camera usually focuses on the center of the screen, but you can specify any area of the screen on which to focus. Tap once to set the focus point, which is represented by a white square (**Figure 5.3**).

The iPad also uses that focus area as the basis to set lighting and white balance. So, for example, if a person in the foreground is silhouetted by a bright background, tap and hold the person to lighten the foreground. You'll see AE/AF Lock appear at the bottom of the screen, which indicates that the exposure and focus are both locked.

Figure 5.3
Specifying focus

Zoom in on a subject

Is the thing you want to photograph a bit too far away? Using the Camera app's digital zoom feature, you can enlarge the image up to five times. Digital zoom works only for capturing still images, not video, and only when shooting with the rear-facing camera.

1. Pinch outward with two fingers, just as you would to zoom in on a photo or Web page. A zoom slider appears at the bottom of the screen.

2. While the slider is visible, you can drag it for more precise zooming. Or, touch and hold the + and – buttons at each end (**Figure 5.4**).

Figure 5.4
Zoom in to get closer.

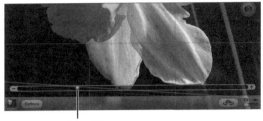

Zoom slider

note Expect the image to degrade when you use the digital zoom feature. Unlike optical zoom, where a telephoto lens moves to enlarge the image, digital zoom accomplishes the resizing solely in software. The processor is making a best-guess estimate of what the image looks like blown up, so the result may be softer than you'd prefer.

Capture Video

Shooting video is similar to capturing still photos.

1. In the Camera app, tap the Photo/Video switch to enter video mode (**Figure 5.5**).

Figure 5.5
Shooting video

Photo/Video switch

note You can tap the screen to set or lock focus and exposure, but video capture doesn't offer the digital zoom feature. However, you can begin recording and then tap to redefine the focus and exposure.

2. Optionally, choose which camera to use by tapping the Camera Switch button.

3. Tap the Record button (which now includes a red recording indicator instead of a camera icon) to start recording.

4. Tap the Record button again to stop.

As with photos, the video you shoot is added to the Camera Roll.

Make FaceTime Calls

Videoconferencing on computers has been around for years—iChat, Skype, and Windows Messenger are just a few options. But as I've learned recently, a toddler's desire to sit in front of a computer screen, even when talking to grandparents, is short-lived. FaceTime on the iPad brings video chatting to wherever you are, and the ability to switch cameras lets you follow your subject around or point to something you want to feature (like the child's latest dance moves).

Set up your FaceTime account

FaceTime uses your Apple ID to identify itself on the network, so other people using FaceTime can connect with you.

1. Open the Settings app and select FaceTime in the left column.

2. Enter your Apple ID and password.

3. Tap the Sign In button.

Once you've entered your Apple ID, you can assign other email addresses (for example, if you don't want to give out your Apple ID to others). Also in the FaceTime settings, tap the Add Another Email button and enter a valid email address. With multiple addresses available, a new Caller ID field appears, which is the address that appears in a friend's copy of FaceTime when you call them. Tap it to choose from your list of addresses.

Set up a FaceTime contact

1. Tap the FaceTime app to open it.

2. Tap the Contacts button to view the people in your Contacts list. If you're just starting out, the list may be empty. Otherwise, if you synced contacts from your computer, they should appear here. I'm assuming here you're starting from scratch; if not, skip ahead to "Make a FaceTime call."

3. Tap the + button to create a new contact.

4. Enter the person's first and last name, phone number (if you know it), and email address (again, if you know it) (**Figure 5.6**).

Figure 5.6
Creating a new FaceTime contact

If the person owns an iPhone 4 or iPhone 4S, they're capable of chatting via FaceTime using their mobile number. Other owners of camera-equipped iPads, or friends who have the FaceTime application installed on their Macs, are identified by their email addresses.

5. Tap Done to finish setting up the contact.

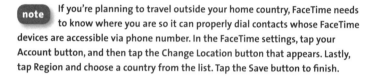 **note** If you're planning to travel outside your home country, FaceTime needs to know where you are so it can properly dial contacts whose FaceTime devices are accessible via phone number. In the FaceTime settings, tap your Account button, and then tap the Change Location button that appears. Lastly, tap Region and choose a country from the list. Tap the Save button to finish.

Make a FaceTime call

1. Tap the Contacts button to view your list of contacts.

2. Tap the name of the person you want to chat with.

3. Tap the person's phone number or email address to initiate a call.

4. When the other person accepts the FaceTime request, you're connected (**Figure 5.7**).

Figure 5.7
*A FaceTime
video chat*

The small window in the corner displays what your camera is sending so you can make sure your face is in the frame. If you wish to move it to another corner, drag it there.

5. To switch between the iPad's two cameras, tap the button at the right in the control bar. You can also mute the audio of your side of the conversation by tapping the Mute button at left.

6. When you're finished with the call, tap the End button to disconnect.

tip Tapping the Mute button only silences the audio; it does not pause the video image. If you want to mute the audio and also pause the image, first tap the Mute button and then press the iPad's Home button to switch to the Home screen. The FaceTime call is still active—you can see a status indicator in the menubar (Figure 5.8)—but your image is frozen to the other person. (If you just exit FaceTime without first tapping the Mute button, you can still talk to the person at the other end of the connection.) Tap the green indicator to return to FaceTime.

Figure 5.8
*A green status
bar indicates
a FaceTime call
is active.*

View recent calls

FaceTime keeps track of previous calls and attempted calls. Tap the Recents button to view them. You can also use this area to add an incoming caller to your list of contacts (**Figure 5.9**, on the next page). Tap the detail button (⊙) next to a person's name to view details about the call. Then tap either the Create New Contact or the Add to Existing Contact button.

Figure 5.9
A recent call log

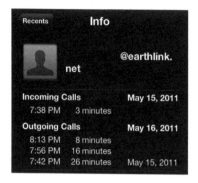

Add a contact to the Favorites list

Rather than search through your contacts for people you frequently call, add them to the Favorites list, accessible by tapping the Favorites button.

1. In the Contacts list, tap the name of a person to view their details.

2. Tap the Add to Favorites button.

3. If there are multiple contact possibilities, such as a mix of phone numbers and email addresses, choose one from the popover that appears.

Or, do the following:

1. Tap the Favorites button to view your Favorites list.

2. Tap the Add (+) button and select a person in your Contacts list.

3. Choose the phone number or email address the person uses for FaceTime. If you've previously participated in a FaceTime chat with them, a blue camera icon appears next to the item.

The person then appears in the Favorites list.

View Photos

Just *look* at that screen! Full color, Retina resolution, larger than a phone, attached to a device that's more comfortable to hold than a laptop. If the iPad didn't already do a thousand other things, you'd think it was designed solely for displaying digital photos.

When you have an iPad stocked with your favorite photos, you have a portable presentation machine. Maybe you want to show off your latest snapshots. Maybe you're a photographer (or real estate agent, or designer, or...) showing a portfolio to a prospective client. Maybe you want to store photos on the iPad while on vacation instead of toting a laptop. Maybe you need to display a slideshow using a projector or on an HDTV. Or maybe you just want to be able to look at your favorite photos whenever you feel like it. The Photos app can deliver your images.

Getting Photos onto the iPad

Where are your photos coming from? You have four options: sync photos from your computer; import photos directly from a camera or memory card using an adapter; send photos to an email account you check on the iPad; or copy pictures from Web pages in Safari.

Sync photos from the computer

With most photos now being captured digitally, it's likely you use photo management software to keep track of them all. Or, you might prefer to organize the image files in a folder on disk. iTunes can handle both.

Sync with photo management software

iTunes recognizes libraries in iPhoto 4.0.3 or later and Aperture 3.0.2 or later on the Mac, and Photoshop Elements 3.0 or later for Windows.

1. Connect the iPad to the computer, open iTunes, and select the iPad in the sidebar.

2. Click the Photos tab.

3. Enable the Sync Photos From option and choose your photo software from the pop-up menu (**Figure 6.1**).

4. To transfer your entire library, choose the first option: All photos, albums, events, and faces.

   Or, enable the second radio button and then mark the checkboxes of any albums, events (or projects, in Aperture), or faces.

note The option to group photos based on events/projects or faces is supported only if you're syncing with iPhoto or Aperture. If you're using Photoshop Elements in Windows, you get the option of syncing all photos and albums or specifying selected albums.

Figure 6.1
*Photos pane
in iTunes*

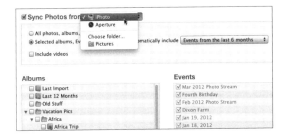

Using the radio button's pop-up menu, you can make some items
appear automatically. For example, regardless of which checkboxes
are selected in the Events or Projects list, you can choose to have the
photos from all events from the last month appear on the iPad.

5. To copy video files located in your library, select the Include Videos
   checkbox.

6. Click the Sync button. iTunes transfers the photos to the iPad.

> **tip** The information in this chapter really only touches on what's possible
> with photos on the iPad. In fact, I wrote an entire book about the
> subject: *The iPad for Photographers*, available from Peachpit Press and your favor-
> ite bookstore. See http://ipadforphotographers.com/ for more information.

Sync with a folder

Some people prefer to manage image files manually or use software—
such as Adobe Photoshop Elements—that organizes and displays photos
in folders. iTunes can use the folder contents, including subfolders, as the
media source for the Photos app.

1. In the Photos pane, choose the Pictures (Mac) or My Pictures
   (Windows) default locations. Or, click Choose Folder and specify a
   different folder.

2. To include everything in the folder, choose the All Folders option. Or, click the Selected Folders button and mark the checkboxes for the folders you wish to sync in the Folders list (**Figure 6.2**).

Figure 6.2
Sync photos from subfolders.

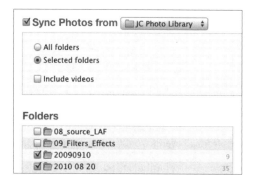

3. Click the Sync button to start the transfer.

tip The iTunes interface is a little confusing on this part. In the previous example, the only photos transferred are the ones in the selected folders (44 pictures). What's not synced are the photos in the parent folder, "JC Photo Library." If I wanted just the images in that folder, and none of the images from the subfolders, I'm out of luck: I'd get either the contents of specific subfolders (Selected Folders option) or everything in "JC Photo Library," subfolders included (All Folders option). So, if you're going to organize photos at the folder level, I recommend storing image files in subfolders, not parent folders.

Import photos from a camera

Using Apple's optional iPad Camera Connection Kit, you don't need iTunes as a middleman for your photos. The kit includes two adapters that connect to the iPad's dock connector: one that accepts SD memory cards and one that accepts a standard USB cable.

tip Wait, did I just say that the iPad can gain a regular USB port? Yes...but there are strings attached. The iPad uses the USB camera connector for transferring image and video files only—but there are a couple of surprises, too. Plug in a USB headset to listen to audio or use a headset's microphone. The benefit of this approach over plugging iPhone-compatible headphones into the iPad's headphone port is the ability to use higher-quality audio electronics. For example, I own a Sennheiser headset that's normally connected to my Mac for Skype calls; I can do the same (using the Skype app) on my iPad now. The other surprise is that the connector recognizes some USB keyboards, which is great if you don't own the iPad Keyboard Dock or a Bluetooth wireless keyboard. (You may need to connect devices through a powered USB hub for them to work.)

To import photos via a camera adapter, do the following:

1. Plug one of the adapters into the iPad.

2. Insert an SD card or plug in a USB cable connected to your camera, depending on which adapter you're using. If the latter, turn on the camera's power.

tip To transfer photos directly from an iPhone, connect the iPhone's sync cable to the USB connector. (Unfortunately, the iPad can't charge the iPhone's battery over this connection, which would be cool in a pinch.)

3. Wake the iPad (and unlock it, if you use a passcode). The Photos app opens and displays the photos on the card or camera.

4. To import all photos, skip to the next step.

   If you'd rather import just some of the images, tap the ones you want; a blue checkmark indicates the ones you've selected (**Figure 6.3**).

Figure 6.3
Selecting photos for import

5. Tap the Import All button at the bottom of the screen to begin copying the files.

   If you made selections in step 4, tap the Import button, which brings up a popover with options to Import All (overriding your selections, in case you changed your mind at the last minute) or Import Selected. Tap one to begin copying the images to the iPad.

   Click the Stop Import button if you want to halt the transfer; doing so doesn't remove any selections you made before importing.

6. When importing is complete, you're given the option to delete or keep the images on the camera or SD card. I advise tapping Keep, and then erasing the card later using the camera's format controls.

7. Remove the SD card or turn off the camera. The transferred photos appear in a new album called Last Import.

tip Photos imported directly from a camera or card can be deleted later by viewing the image and tapping the Trash button (🗑). To turn the picture 90 degrees counterclockwise, if necessary, tap the Edit button and then the Rotate button.

Import photos from email

Do you have a family member who likes to send photos via email? Rather than digging through your old messages to view those photos later, add them to the iPad's photo collection.

1. In the Mail app, open the message containing the photo attachments.

2. Touch and hold a photo to bring up a popover containing actions you can take (**Figure 6.4**).

3. Tap the Save Image button. Or, if several images are included, tap the Save *[number]* Images button. The photos are added to the Camera Roll album in the Photos app.

Figure 6.4
Saving images from Mail

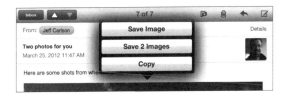

Import photos from other apps

The ability to save images from Mail also applies to other apps. In Safari, for example, touch and hold any image and then tap Save Image to store it. However, keep in mind that images on the Web don't have the same high resolution as ones you'd import from your digital camera, so they may not look as good when expanded to fill the iPad's screen.

View Photos

We've covered all the ways to get photos onto the iPad, but that's just preamble for viewing them.

View a photo

Open the Photos app and tap the Photos button at the top of the screen to see thumbnails of all the photos stored on the iPad. Tap a photo to open it.

The onscreen controls disappear after a few seconds so you can enjoy just the image. Rotate the iPad to match the photo's orientation for the best effect (**Figure 6.5**, on the next page).

Figure 6.5
A photo viewed widescreen

While viewing an image, you can do a number of things:

- Tap once anywhere to make the controls reappear. Tap again to make them go away again, or wait a few seconds.

- Double-tap anywhere on the photo to zoom in. Double-tapping again zooms back out to fit.

- To zoom with more control, pinch two fingers outward. Swipe anywhere on the image to view a different area of the photo. To zoom back out, pinch two fingers together or double-tap the screen.

- To quickly skim all of the photos, tap once to view the controls and then drag the navigation bar at the bottom of the screen (**Figure 6.6**). The preview is extremely fast because the Photos app displays low-resolution images as you drag, giving you a sense of what the photo is without having to draw all of the detail. If you pause, the higher-resolution version appears.

- Tap the button at the upper-left corner (which displays the name of the current album) to return to the Photos pane.

Figure 6.6
Quickly navigating photos

Drag along strip.

View a collection

In addition to the big free-for-all that is the Photos pane, your images are also organized into collections. These can be albums, events, or faces, depending on the software on your computer. Each type is a different way of categorizing the photos, but the controls are the same.

1. Tap the Albums, Events, or Faces button to switch to that pane (if the option is available).

2. Pinch outward with two fingers on a collection you want to open. As you do so, the photos within unstack themselves so you can preview what you're about to open (**Figure 6.7**). If it's not the set you were expecting, just pinch your fingers together to return the collection to its stacked state.

Figure 6.7
Previewing a collection

Before

Pinched outward

3. When you've expanded a collection far enough, it takes over the entire screen. Tap a photo thumbnail to view the image.

tip I'm a big fan of useless shortcuts—things that were implemented just because they could be—and here's a great one. Instead of just tapping a thumbnail to view the photo full screen, use the expanding pinch gesture to enlarge it. Now, before you let go, *rotate your fingers*. The image can be freely rotated and scaled as long as your fingers are touching the glass. Why? I couldn't tell you. Maybe to preview a landscape photo in portrait orientation without rotating the iPad. Or maybe because the graphics capabilities inside the iPad can do it, and that's a good enough reason. I don't know, but it's fun to play with.

tip I think this is my favorite Photos tip: Instead of trying to tap the back button in the upper-left corner of the screen (which is labeled with the name of the enclosing folder), pinch two fingers together to collapse the stack you're currently viewing. It's much faster, because your fingers are likely already in place from opening a stack or zooming in on an image.

tip To change the photo used for someone's Faces collection, go to iPhoto or Aperture and switch to the Faces view. Move your mouse pointer over the person's image to preview their photos, and find one you want. If you're in iPhoto, double-click the photo to view all photos associated with that name; if you're in Aperture, you don't need to take that extra step. Next, right-click or Control-click the photo and choose Set Key Photo. Sync again to apply the change.

View photos in Places

The Photos app offers one more type of collection, and it works a bit differently than the others. A Places pane appears if any of your images include location tags—GPS coordinates marking where the photos were shot, either written to the file when captured (the iPhone can do this, as can some GPS add-on devices for some cameras) or applied in iPhoto, Aperture, Photoshop Elements, or other software.

When you tap the Places button, you see a map that features red pins marking where photos were taken. Tap a pin to view a stack (**Figure 6.8**). As with other collections, pinch or tap the stack to view its photos.

Figure 6.8
*Photos with
location
information*

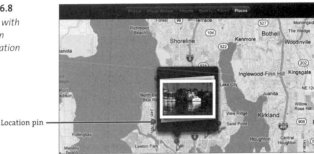

Location pin

Edit photos

The Photos app offers a few basic editing features for quick adjustments.

1. With a photo open, tap the Edit button.

2. Do one of the following:

   ■ Tap the Rotate button to turn the image counterclockwise in 90-degree increments. This is useful when a photo's correct orientation wasn't picked up during import.

   ■ Tap the Enhance button to let the Photos app adjust exposure and color as it sees fit.

   ■ If someone in the photo suffers from red-eye, tap the Red-Eye button and then tap the affected eyes.

   ■ To adjust the visible area of the photo, tap the Crop button and drag a corner handle or edge; drag the center of the crop area to reposition it. After you resize the crop area, tap the Constrain button to choose an aspect ratio to enforce. If the photo needs straightening, use two fingers to zoom and then rotate as needed. Tap the Crop button to make the change stick.

3. When you're done making edits, tap the Save button and then the Save to Camera Roll button. The app saves a new, edited version of the photo. Or, you can discard the edits by tapping the Revert to Original button.

Even after you've edited a photo, the Photos app remembers the original. So you can always open the edited version, tap the Edit button, and then tap the Revert to Original button.

> **tip** Want more editing capability? A lot more? Apple's iPhoto for iOS is an impressive app for making detailed adjustments to photos without leaving the iPad. It's available from the App Store for $4.99.

Play a video

Most digital cameras now shoot video as well as stills, so the Photos app can play video, too. In iTunes, make sure you enable the Include Videos option in the Photos pane. The iPad Camera Connection Kit also allows you to import videos you've shot directly into the iPad. Some cameras' video may not play, though. When you come across a video clip in the Photos app, do any of the following:

- Tap the Play button that appears in the middle of the screen to start playing. Or, you can tap the Play button in the toolbar (**Figure 6.9**).

- Touch and hold the playhead to skim through the filmstrip and locate a particular section of the video. If you hold for a moment, the filmstrip spreads out horizontally to give you finer control while skimming.

- While the video is playing, tap the Pause button (■) to stop playback.

Figure 6.9
Viewing
video clips

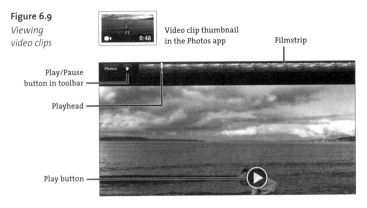

Video clip thumbnail
in the Photos app

Filmstrip

Play/Pause
button in toolbar

Playhead

Play button

> **tip** A video in the Photos app benefits from the photo controls, which means you can pinch to zoom a video while it's playing.

> **tip** Here's a cool side effect of playing videos in the Photos app. Using the iPad Camera Connection Kit, you can import movies—the Hollywood kind—and watch them on the iPad. For example, if you're going on vacation and you don't want to bring a laptop, but the number of movies you want to watch won't fit on the iPad's internal storage, load up on some inexpensive SD memory cards. Using a program such as HandBrake (www.handbrake.fr) on your computer, digitize your DVDs to digital M4V files. Copy those to one or more SD memory cards, then insert one into the memory card adapter. Transfer a movie to the iPad in the Photos app and then watch it there. (It won't show up in the Videos app.) When you're done, delete the movie and transfer another one. However, there's a catch: The video file must be named something similar to what a digital camera would use. The Photos app won't recognize a file named "Star Wars.MP4", but it will play "IMG_1234.MP4".

> **tip** Another way to beat the limitation of the iPad's internal storage— especially if you bought the 16 GB model and are bumping up against its limit—is to buy an external wireless hard disk, such as the Seagate GoFlex Satellite. It acts as a portable wireless server, enabling you to stream photos or movies over Wi-Fi. It's great for a long vacation involving lots of movies.

View a Slideshow

Swiping is fine for showing off a few pictures, but there are times when you'll want the iPad to drive a photo presentation. In that case, set up an impromptu slideshow of one of your albums.

1. Open a collection in any of the panes, or go to the Photos pane if you want to play back all of your pictures in the slideshow.

2. Tap the Slideshow button. The Slideshow Options popover appears (**Figure 6.10**).

Figure 6.10
Slideshow options

3. If you want music to play during the slideshow, set the Play Music switch to On. If not, make sure the option is off and skip the next step.

4. Tap the Music button to choose which music to use. The popover becomes a compact version of the music list in the Music app, where you can navigate your music library by song title, artist, album, play-list, and other criteria.

note Surprisingly, the Photos app lets you play *only one song* during a slideshow—not a playlist, not an album, just one song. Even more mind-bending is that this behavior has never changed, even through several major releases of iOS.

5. Tap the Transitions button and choose a transition style to use.

6. Tap the Start Slideshow button. If you need to cancel the slideshow while it's playing, tap once anywhere on the screen.

The slideshow plays until all photos have been displayed or until the music ends. However, you can customize a few of the slideshow parameters. Go to Settings > Photos, where you can specify how long each slide appears onscreen (in increments from 2 to 20 seconds), whether the photos (and music) repeat after they've initially appeared, and whether the order should be shuffled. These settings apply to any slideshow you run in the Photos app.

> **tip** The Photos app respects the order in which the pictures were sorted before you synced them. If you want a custom order, set it up in your photo software.

> **tip** What do you do with an iPad when you're not using it? Instead of setting it down on a table or a stack of mail, put that big screen to use as a picture frame. To activate the feature, simply press the Picture Frame button that appears to the right of the Slide to Unlock control on the lock screen. While remaining locked, the screen switches into a slideshow mode. Tap the screen and then tap the button again to exit the Picture Frame mode. You can change some aspects of how the slideshow is presented by going to Settings > Picture Frame.

Share Photos

On more than one occasion I've shown a photo to someone who then said, "Ooh, can you send that to me?" Why yes, I certainly can, and it's easy to do.

The Photos app features several methods of getting photos off the device.

Share one photo via email

To attach a photo to an outgoing message, do the following:

1. Open a photo and tap the Action button (📤).

2. In the popover that appears, tap Email Photo. A new outgoing mail message appears.

3. Add a recipient, a subject, and optional message text.

4. Tap the Send button to dispatch the photo.

Share multiple photos via email

It's possible to group several photos into an email message.

1. In the Photos app, tap a collection to open it.

2. Tap the Action button (📤).

3. Tap the photos you wish to send. Selected ones are marked with a blue checkmark (**Figure 6.11**).

Figure 6.11
Selecting multiple photos for sharing

4. Tap the Share button.

5. From the popover that appears, tap the Email button to create a new outgoing message with the photos as attachments.

6. Address the message and tap the Send button.

tip Many photo sharing services, like Flickr (www.flickr.com), accept uploads via email. You're given a personal Flickr email address, and any image files sent to that address are posted to your photostream.

note Although sending files via email is convenient, I don't recommend ganging up a bunch of images together in one message. That increases the chance that a mail server might think you're sending spam or viruses; or your recipient may not have the bandwidth to deal with such large messages.

Print a photo

If you're connected wirelessly to a supported printer, choose Print from the Action popover to print a copy of the photo. To print more than one photo, tap the Action button, tap the Share button, and then choose Print. (See Chapter 1 for more on printing.)

Copy a photo

To copy the image to the iPad's temporary memory, choose Copy Photo from the Action popover. When viewing a collection, you can also touch and hold a photo thumbnail and choose Copy.

Or, with multiple images selected, tap the Copy button in the toolbar. After copying the photo, you can paste it elsewhere, such as in another app or in an email message.

Assign a photo to a contact

If you have a photo of a friend whose information is in your Contacts app, choose the Assign to Contact option from the Action popover. Select the person's name in the Contacts list that appears, then pinch and drag to position the photo in the frame. Tap the Use button to assign the photo.

Use a photo as wallpaper

Chapter 2 covers how to set wallpapers in the iPad's Settings app, but in Photos you can do it directly. Choose Use as Wallpaper from the Action popover, then choose Set Lock Screen, Set Home Screen, or Set Both.

View photos on a TV or projector

For a real big-screen slideshow experience, display your photos on an HDTV or a digital projector. The iPad offers two ways to do it: sharing via AirPlay, or connected by special video cables.

Using AirPlay

If you own an Apple TV or other AirPlay-enabled video device, you can send photos to your television wirelessly.

1. Tap a photo to view it on the iPad.

2. Tap the AirPlay button (**Figure 6.12**).

Figure 6.12
*Choosing an
AirPlay device*

3. Tap the name of the AirPlay device. The AirPlay button turns blue to indicate it's active, and your photo appears on the television. You can swipe to view other photos, or tap the Slideshow button to start a slideshow. Tap anywhere on the screen to stop the slideshow.

Using a video cable

A number of adapters and cables enable you to connect the iPad to a television. Apple's Digital AV Adapter connects the iPad via HDMI; the Apple VGA Adapter works with older VGA connections, as found on many projectors; and the Apple Component AV Cable and Composite AV Cable work with devices using those connectors.

Sync imported photos and videos back to the computer

You probably don't intend to keep photos you imported using the iPad Camera Connection Kit in the iPad's memory. When you get back to your computer, do the following to move them to its hard drive:

1. Connect the iPad to the computer.

2. Open your photo management software.

3. Use the software's feature for importing photos, just as if you'd attached a camera.

   The computer sees the iPad as a USB storage device. Under Windows, you can view it as you would view an attached disk. On the Mac, you need to use the photo software or the Image Capture application to access the iPad's pictures.

4. After importing the files, delete them from the iPad: Open a collection, tap the Action button (), tap to select the images you want to remove, and then tap the Delete button. Tap the Delete Selected Photos button that appears (to confirm your action).

Use iCloud Photo Stream

When the Photo Stream feature of iCloud is enabled, images you capture using the iPad (or an iPhone or iPod touch) appear in the Photos app. Enable the Photo Stream option in Settings > iCloud.

Photo Stream automatically keeps 1000 photos, including the last 30 days' worth of new photos. If you run across a photo you want to keep on the iPad (before it's rotated out by new photos), add it to the Camera Roll or to an album, as follows:

1. In the Photos app, tap the Photo Stream button to view your stream.

2. Tap the Action button (⬆).

3. Select the photo or photos you wish to keep.

4. Tap the Save button.

5. Tap Save to Camera Roll, Save to Existing Album, or Save to New Album (**Figure 6.13**).

Figure 6.13
Copying a Photo Stream photo to an album

Similarly, you can delete photos from your Photo Stream. With one or more photos selected, as in the steps above, tap the Delete button. Tap the Delete Selected Photos button that appears to confirm that you want to remove the images from all devices that share your Photo Stream.

7

Read Books and Magazines

Under other circumstances, the subject of reading electronic books on a device would warrant a few paragraphs or maybe an extended sidebar. But the iPad's handheld form factor and large storage capacity makes it an attractive ebook reader. It wouldn't surprise me if some people view the iPad primarily as an ebook reader that also happens to do other stuff.

Instead of packing a tote bag bursting with hardcovers on your next vacation, Apple's iBooks app offers an attractive alternative: Store digital versions of books on the iPad, and connect to the iBookstore to buy new ones when you need more. And ebooks aren't just plain text anymore—the iBookstore offers illustrated works including children's picture books and fine arts books as well as titles with embedded video.

In addition to purchased books, the iBooks app can also store Adobe Acrobat PDF files, enabling you to read titles from the wide swath of publishers who don't publish in the EPUB format that iBooks uses.

Note that although this chapter focuses on the features of the iBooks app, that's not the only player out there. If you prefer to buy ebooks from Amazon, the free Kindle app reads titles from the online retailer; and if you previously owned a physical Kindle e-reader, you can keep your existing library.

The iPad can also handle other types of electronic text, with a multitude of media companies offering digital versions of magazines and newspapers, most accessed in standalone apps or viewed in Safari.

Install the iBooks App

The iBooks app isn't included on the iPad by default. In iTunes or using the App Store on the iPad, search for "iBooks." Download and install the free app.

 The iBooks app is available to all international markets that have an App Store. However, the content available in the iBookstore varies from country to country.

Browse Your Library

When you open it, iBooks displays your books arranged on a faux wooden shelf (**Figure 7.1**). Swipe up to reveal more books as your library grows.

tip **Swipe down as far as you can to reveal a little hidden surprise carved in the back panel of the bookshelf.**

Icon or List view

Figure 7.1
*The iBooks
bookshelf*

Manage collections

Imagine a real-world library where all the books are stacked haphazardly
in the middle of the floor. That's what the iBooks library could become,
if not for collections and controls for organizing the titles. Right away,
iBooks includes two collections: Books, for EPUB files; and PDFs, for files in
Portable Document Format. If you've added any PDF files to iBooks, view
them by doing one of the following:

- Tap the Collections button, then tap the PDFs button to see them
  arranged on another shelf (**Figure 7.2**).

- Swipe right or left to switch between collection shelves.

Figure 7.2
*Getting to the
PDF shelf*

note Adding PDFs to your iTunes library is easy—simply drag and drop from
your desktop into the iTunes application and they're automatically
added to iBooks. You can also send PDFs to iBooks from the Mail app on the
iPad: Touch and hold the PDF file in an email, choose the Open In menu item,
and then select iBooks from the list of compatible apps.

Rearrange or remove titles

Normally, books and PDFs appear in the order you add them to the library, with the most recent title appearing at the top-left location. You can move them around easily: Touch and hold a title, and drag it to a new spot.

To delete titles, do the following:

1. Tap the Edit button.

2. Select one or more titles by tapping their covers (which gain blue checkmarks).

3. Tap the red Delete button (you'll be asked to confirm this deletion).

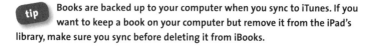 **Books are backed up to your computer when you sync to iTunes. If you want to keep a book on your computer but remove it from the iPad's library, make sure you sync before deleting it from iBooks.**

Organize titles into collections

Collections let you do more than just separate books and PDFs—you can create multiple shelves based on whatever organizing criteria you come up with. For instance, you could separate biographies, science fiction, and historical romances on their own sets of shelves. To create a new collection, do the following:

1. Tap the Collections button, and then tap the New button.

2. Type a name in the blank field that appears, then tap Done (**Figure 7.3**).

Tapping the Edit button in the popover enables you to reorder or delete collections (although Books and PDFs can't be altered).

To view a collection, tap the Collections button and then tap that collection's name. Or, swipe left or right to switch among them.

Figure 7.3
*Creating a
new collection*

> **tip** Despite the two default camps for books and PDFs, collections are
> agnostic as far as file format, allowing you to place books and PDFs
> side by side on a shelf.

Move titles to collections

After you've set up some collections, moving titles between them is similar to the steps for deleting books.

1. Tap the Edit button.

2. Tap to select the titles you wish to move.

3. Tap the Move button (**Figure 7.4**).

4. Tap the collection name to set the destination for the move. (You can
   also create a new collection at this step if you thought of a new cate-
   gorization.) iBooks moves the titles and whisks you to that collection.

Figure 7.4
*Moving selected
titles to other
collections*

tip If you delete a title from a collection and then later decide to sync it back to your iPad, it will return to that collection. Also, if you delete a collection, you'll be asked whether you want to remove titles on that shelf from the iPad or move them to their original collection.

note Keep the same collections across multiple iOS devices by turning on Sync Collections in Settings > iBooks.

Browse in List view

Should any of your collections get too full of titles, or you want a sorted view, tap the List view button (**Figure 7.5**).

Figure 7.5
Sort options in List view

List view presents more options for organizing the library. Tap one of the buttons at the bottom of the screen to reorder the list.

tip Titles in the Bookshelf List view can be reordered, deleted, and moved to different collections, just as they can in the main Bookshelf view.

tip To delete a book quickly in List view, swipe its title left to right (or right to left) and then tap the Delete button that appears.

Search for books

When the number of books in your library starts to get really out of control (or, as my stepsister would say, "A good start"), you can use the

Search Books field hidden at the top of both the Bookshelf and List views to locate a title. Swipe down until you reach the top to reveal the Search field in either view, tap inside the field, and then start typing a title or author name to narrow the list (**Figure 7.6**).

Figure 7.6
Searching your library

Read Books and PDFs

To open a book, tap its cover. The appearance of the book changes based on the iPad's rotation. When viewed in portrait orientation, you see one page at a time. Turn it to landscape orientation and the text is split over two pages.

> **tip** To get you started, Apple offers a free book—The Beatles' *Yellow Submarine*, as I write this. If you're not prompted after installing iBooks for the first time, go to the iBookstore, scroll to the bottom of the Featured page, and tap the Free Book link. Or, go to the iTunes Store and click Free Book in the Quick Links sidebar.

> **tip** To keep the screen from rotating if you shift or change position, use your chosen method of locking the rotation—either double-pressing the Home button and swiping to the left, or using the side switch above the volume controls. (See Chapter 1 to learn how to configure the side switch.)

Navigate a book

It feels a little funny that I should tell you how to read a book (obviously, you're doing a fine job reading my book), but there are a few things to note before you get absorbed by the content you're about to read.

- Tap the middle of the screen to reveal the reading controls if they're not visible. (Tap again to make them disappear.)

- To turn to the next page, swipe right to left. Swipe left to right to go to the previous page. You don't need to swipe the width of the page; a small swipe works the same.

  For kicks, drag the page edge slowly (**Figure 7.7**): Apple made a point of reproducing the look of curling the page, complete with a preview of what's on the next page (in landscape mode) or ghosted, reversed letters that would show through typical book-quality paper.

- Tap the right or left edge of the screen to turn the page using a faster, minimal animation.

Figure 7.7
Turning pages

Tap for previous page.   Tap for next page.

tip In the iBooks preferences (go to Settings > iBooks) is the option to specify what happens when you tap the left margin. By default it takes you to the previous page, but if you don't anticipate going backwards (you forward-thinking reader, you), tap the Tap Left Margin button and choose Next Page instead of Previous Page. You can still go to the previous page by swiping left-to-right anywhere on the screen.

- Tap the Contents button (≡) to view the table of contents. You can tap a chapter or section to navigate to it, or tap the Resume button to go back to where you were.

- Drag the navigation control at the bottom of the screen to jump to a specific page or chapter (**Figure 7.8**).

Figure 7.8
Advancing to another section of the book

note I love that the lower-right corner tells you how many pages are left in the current chapter. How many times have you been reading in bed, almost at the verge of sleep, but decided to push on until the end of the chapter? In iBooks, you don't have to flip ahead to see how much further ahead the next chapter is.

Navigate an illustrated book

iBooks can render fully illustrated books—such as children's picture books or fine art books—reproducing the "spread" layout of the original paper version, where illustrations can span across two opened pages. The free *Yellow Submarine* book is fully illustrated—and animated, too.

While most of the navigation tools are similar to text-based titles, illustrated books get a few navigation enhancements:

- The navigation control at the bottom of the screen displays page previews rather than just page numbers. Tap it to reveal a larger popover preview, and drag to jump to a new page (**Figure 7.9**).

- Tap the Contents button to also view page previews.

- Double-tap to get a closer look at a page.

- Pinch with two fingers to zoom in and out.

Figure 7.9
Navigating an
illustrated book

Navigate a PDF

Reading a PDF in iBooks is a bit like reading an illustrated book (minus the page curling effect when you turn a page), but with a few differences.

- The navigation control at the bottom of the screen displays small thumbnails of the pages, but you don't get a larger preview popover.

- The reading controls at the top of the page are similar to books, save for the addition of an Action button, enabling you to attach the PDF to an email or send it to a printer.

note Unlike with books, you won't get a two-page spread when viewing a PDF in landscape view. However, you'll have more control over page display if you use another PDF-compatible app, such as GoodReader.

Reading Books Aloud with VoiceOver

The iPad includes VoiceOver, an accessibility feature for people with limited vision that reads aloud text and the names of onscreen elements. It's also a way to have iBooks read a book to me while I'm cooking, driving, or otherwise wanting a textbook to act like an audiobook. When iBooks was first introduced, the VoiceOver feature was limited to reading back just one page at a time in its synthesized voice. However, that limitation has been lifted and reading now flows automatically from one page to the next.

To use VoiceOver, you'll have to do a little system-wide preference setup and learn a few new gestures to control the iPad. (I've also found it doesn't work in all books.) To give it a try, do the following:

1. In Settings > General > Accessiblity > VoiceOver, tap the VoiceOver switch to On.

2. In a book within iBooks, tap once anywhere in the text and then flick up with two fingers to begin reading the page. When the end of the page is reached, it turns automatically and continues reading the next page.

3. To pause at any time, tap the screen with two fingers. Tapping again with two fingers restarts the reading.

Search Text

Another way to navigate a book or PDF is to look for occurrences of specific text (or, I suppose, another way to find out how many times an author swears throughout the text). The number of matches appears at the bottom of the results list. This feature also provides convenient Search Google and Search Wikipedia buttons to expand your search in Safari.

1. Tap the middle of the screen to display the reading controls.

2. Tap the Search button (Q) in the upper-right corner.

3. Type a search term, and tap the Search button on the onscreen keyboard or wait a few seconds for results to appear (**Figure 7.10**).

4. Scroll through the results to find the one you want, and then tap it to go to that place in the book. The term is highlighted so you can find it easily.

Figure 7.10
Searching the book

tip When you tap the Search button again, the previous results are still available.

A slightly faster method of searching is available when you select a word or phrase on a page.

1. Touch and hold to select the text you want to find.

2. From the options that appear, tap the Search button (**Figure 7.11**). The search results popover appears.

Figure 7.11
*Searching
by selection*

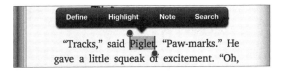

Change Appearance

Reading is a personal experience, and iBooks offers a few options for customizing the appearance of your books and PDFs.

Adjust screen brightness

The iPad's bright screen becomes a liability when it's flooding the bedroom with light and preventing your partner from sleeping or when it's intimidating the pets. Tap the Appearance button ($_A$A) to expose a slider that changes the brightness level (**Figure 7.12**).

Figure 7.12
*The Brightness
slider*

note The Brightness setting in iBooks is applied system-wide, so it sticks when you leave the iBooks app. To bring the backlight level back up after leaving iBooks, double-press the Home button and then swipe to the right to access brightness controls (or, open Settings > Brightness & Wallpaper).

Change text size and font

One noticeable advantage of electronic books is that you can adjust the type size to match what's comfortable for your eyes.

1. Tap the Appearance button (ₐA) to display a popover with text options (**Figure 7.13**).

Figure 7.13
Adjusting text size and font

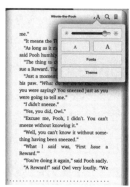

2. Tap the small A button to make the text smaller, or tap the large A button to make it larger.

3. Tap the Fonts button to reveal the typeface options.

4. Tap one of the font names to use that for the book's text.

5. Tap outside the popover to dismiss it.

> **tip** If you feel more comfortable reading larger fonts, go to the iBooks preferences and turn off Full Justification to render text with a ragged right edge—which should improve readability at increased point sizes. If you keep Full Justification turned on, it's best to also keep Auto-hyphenation on to avoid some lines from having too much space.

> **tip** Another way to turn down the bright backlighting of the white page background is to change the theme. Tap the Theme button and enable the Sepia (cream) or Night (reversed) option. Here you can also choose to turn on Full Screen mode, which dispenses with the faux book borders.

Use Bookmarks, Highlights, and Notes

iBooks offers a full toolset for jogging your memory after you've put the
ebook down, including bookmarks, text highlighting, and the ability to
add notes in the virtual page margins.

note For highlighting and note-taking capabilities in PDFs, you'll need to
turn to an alternative app, such as GoodReader. See "Other Ebook
Readers," later in this chapter.

Create a new bookmark

1. On a page with text you want to remember later, tap the Bookmark
button (📑).

2. Depending on what format you're reading, the bookmark appears
differently:

   - For EPUB ebooks, a red bookmark ribbon slides over the page's
Bookmark button. The ribbon stays on the page even when the
reading controls disappear.

   - In illustrated books and PDFs, the red bookmark isn't visible on the
page once the reading controls disappear. However, if you tap the
Contents button, you'll see the red bookmark on those thumbnail
previews that have been bookmarked.

To remove a bookmark, simply tap the ribbon (or ribbon button) and it
goes away.

Create a new highlight

Because text gets reflowed when you switch between portrait and landscape views, your bookmark placement might not end up where you
thought it would go.

A more precise way to recall text or illustrations is to use the highlighting feature.

1. Touch and hold to select the text or illustration you want to highlight. By default, a single word or image is selected. Drag the selection handles to expand what you'll highlight.

2. From the options that appear, tap the Highlight button. The selected text is then colored like it was drawn over with a real highlighter pen.

3. The options change to reveal the colors available (**Figure 7.14**); tap a color or the button to underline the selection.

Figure 7.14
Highlighting text

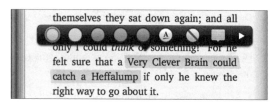

Change highlight coloring

1. Tap on text or an image that's been highlighted.

2. From the options that appear, tap the color to use.

tip I like to categorize things by color, so the fact that you can change highlight colors makes me happy (as does the highlighter pen rendering). I'm sure the point is to simply let you choose your favorite color, but I can imagine two people sharing an iPad using colored bookmarks to read the same book. Or marking up text for different categories in a textbook, for example.

tip Tapping on highlighted material also brings up the option to Remove Highlight—something that was impossible to do in your old college textbooks.

Create a new note

If something sparks an idea for next month's book club gathering, you can mark up your electronic book with notes. The process is similar to highlighting, except you get to add a virtual Post-it note to the page.

1. Touch and hold to select text or an illustration.

2. Tap the Note button from the options that appear. A square notepad appears, allowing you to type as long or as succinctly as you wish.

3. Tap outside the note when finished. A small colored note is added to the margin (**Figure 7.15**).

Figure 7.15
*A note in
the margin*

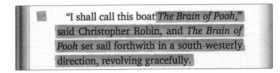

> "I shall call this boat *The Brain of Pooh*," said Christopher Robin, and *The Brain of Pooh* set sail forthwith in a south-westerly direction, revolving gracefully.

Return to a bookmark, highlight, or note

When it's time to return to a placemarker or review your highlighting and notes, do the following:

1. Tap the Contents button to view the table of contents.

2. Tap the Bookmarks or Notes button.

3. Tap a bookmark, highlight, or note from the list to go to that page (**Figure 7.16**).

Figure 7.16
Notes list

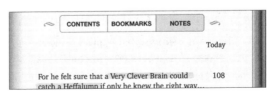

CONTENTS	BOOKMARKS	NOTES

Today

For he felt sure that a Very Clever Brain could   108
catch a Heffalump if only he knew the right way...

Tap the Action button at the top of the Bookmarks list to print any notes or to share them via email.

 Make sure your bookmarks, highlights, and notes are synchronized across all of your iOS devices by turning on Sync Bookmarks in Settings > iBooks.

Look Up Word Definitions

One of the great joys (and sometimes great frustrations) of reading is coming across unfamiliar words. iBooks offers a built-in dictionary lookup feature.

1. Touch and hold a word to select it.

2. From the options that appear, tap the Dictionary button. A definition appears (**Figure 7.17**).

Figure 7.17
*Viewing a
definition*

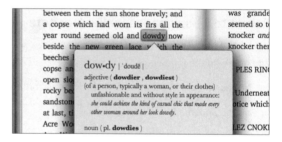

Buy Books from the iBookstore

This will come as a surprise, but Apple is ready and eager to sell you more electronic books in its iBookstore. The store is available only from within the iBooks app, but it uses your iTunes Store account.

To access the iBookstore from your library, tap the Store button. In a great bit of visual flair, the library rotates as if the store were a hidden passage-way behind the bookcase (**Figure 7.18**).

Figure 7.18
*"Put...the...
candle...back!"*

The library rotates...   ...to reveal the iBookstore.

Browsing the iBookstore is similar to shopping at the iTunes Store.

- Tap a book title to view more information about it (**Figure 7.19**).

Figure 7.19
*Viewing more
info about a book*

- To purchase the book, tap the price button, which changes to read "Buy Book." Tap the button again to buy the book, which, after you enter your account and password, downloads to your library.

- Tap the Get Sample button to download a sample (usually the first chapter or a sizable excerpt). It appears in your library with a Sample banner on the cover (**Figure 7.20**). If you like the book, tap the Buy button that appears at the top of the screen or at the end of the sample.

Figure 7.20
A sample of a book

Buy title from within the sample.

Sample banner

tip Tap the Categories button at the top of the iBookstore screen to locate books in various genres. You can also browse the *New York Times* best-seller list by tapping the NYTimes button in the toolbar.

tip You don't have to shell out money to get a taste of iBooks titles. Tap the Browse button at the iBookstore and then tap the Free button to view books.

note Books purchased from the iBookstore are protected by Apple's FairPlay digital rights management (DRM) scheme, which means you can't give the book to someone else when you're finished reading it, as you can with a print book. That also adds an unfortunate (and stupid) limitation: You can't copy any selected text in a book purchased from the store.

Import Your Own Ebooks

Books from the iBookstore are formatted as EPUB files, an open format designed for electronic publishing by the International Digital Publishing Forum. Titles from Project Gutenberg (www.gutenberg.org) are all EPUB files, without Apple's DRM, and are available from other sources.

If you purchase or download an EPUB file, you can add the book to your iBooks library. In iTunes, drag the file to the Library section in the sidebar or to the iTunes application icon; you can also choose File > Add to Library and locate the file. The book is added to the iPad the next time you sync.

Creating Your Own EPUB Books

Writing a novel? Or perhaps you have an electronic book formatted as a text-only file? With the assistance of a few utilities, you can build your own EPUB files for viewing in iBooks (or any other reader that accepts the format). Here are a few examples:

- Pages, from Apple's iWork (www.apple.com/iwork/), allows you to export any document into the EPUB format for reading in iBooks.

- iBooks Author (www.apple.com/ibooks-author/) is Apple's free Mac OS X app for developing media-rich textbooks and similar types of titles.

- Calibre (www.calibre-ebook.com) is an application available for Windows, Mac OS X, and Linux that accepts several text formats and converts a document to an EPUB.

- Storyist (www.storyist.com) for Mac OS X includes support for outputting EPUB files, including adding images.

- Adobe InDesign (www.adobe.com) is the big gorilla in this zoo, with support for creating EPUB files.

note Before you purchase EPUB books online, make sure you know what you're buying. Not every EPUB file will work with iBooks. Titles from Kobo (www.kobobooks.com), for example, are EPUB formatted but are protected by Adobe DRM. (You can download the free Kobo app to read them.)

Other Ebook Readers

iBooks is the Apple-designed option, but of course a plethora of other ebook reading applications are out there (such as a little Amazon.com offering you may have heard of). Publishers are also writing iPad *apps*, not just book files, that do so much more than turn pages.

- **Kindle for iPad.** When people think of Amazon's Kindle, they picture the hardware: slim devices with grayscale E Ink screens that store lots of ebooks and have great battery life. What they may forget is that Amazon offers Kindle for iPad, a free app that brings the reading experience to the iPad. It's a great alternative if you're already using Amazon for purchases.

- **Barnes & Noble Nook.** Barnes & Noble got into the e-reader market with its Nook devices and multi-platform software, including two apps for the iPad. The Nook for iPad app differentiates itself with more choices for text rendering and layout. You can customize both text and page colors and save those combinations as themes, as well as modify leading (the space between lines) and margins. Barnes & Noble was also the first company to allow you to lend titles to others who have Nook devices or software, though not every title is available to lend (it's up to the publisher to decide); Amazon has followed suit with a similar two-week lending feature.

  While iBooks now offers children's picture books, the Nook Kids app is dedicated exclusively to this genre. And some books can read to your toddler (with a more human-sounding voice than the iPad's VoiceOver feature). Look for titles carrying the Nook Kids Read to Me marker on the Barnes & Noble Web site.

- **Ebooks from public libraries.** Voracious library users might feel a shock to the pocketbook, as the switch from free borrowing to ebook ownership can put a dent in the entertainment budget. But there's hope for the book hungry, as more libraries are now lending ebooks.

   Bluefire Reader (www.bluefirereader.com/bluefire-reader.html) reads files protected by Adobe DRM. OverDrive Media Console (www.overdrive.com) ties into a network of libraries.

- **Standalone apps.** Publishers also offer standalone apps for books that include not only the core text, but other multimedia content. For example, many children's books have options to read the story aloud, play games, and color on the screen. Reference works, such as *The Elements: A Visual Exploration*, can convey much more information than the facts and some photos.

- **Comic books.** Since its release, I can't tell you how many reviewers (myself included) have pointed out that the iPad could be the enticement that makes them start reading comics again. Apps like Marvel, DC, iVerse, and IDW provide the framework for reading and then let you purchase issues in the app. Apple has now started offering graphic novels in the iBookstore, too.

- **Read PDF files and more with GoodReader.** Download the reader to rule them all. GoodReader (www.goodiware.com) is one of those apps that does so much you feel like you're scratching the surface. A more powerful PDF viewer than iBooks, GoodReader offers more options for viewing PDFs (including orientation adjustment and double pages) and can mark up pages (from highlighting and notes to drawing figures and underlining text).

In addition to viewing these static files, you can also play a wide range of video and audio files as well as view Web archives (which bundle all text and images from Web pages and preserve their original layout) saved from Safari on your Mac or Windows PC.

You can import files by using the drag-and-drop interface in the Apps pane within iTunes, by transferring files over a Wi-Fi network, by downloading from the Web, and even by accessing your Dropbox account. It preserves Web links, lets you add bookmarks, allows you to password-protect files, and so much more than I have room to go into here.

Read Magazines with Newsstand

Do your reading tastes veer more toward magazines? Newsstand provides an interface for getting and reading iPad versions of popular magazines. Tap the Newsstand icon to reveal magazines (**Figure 7.21**), and tap the Store button to locate others.

Figure 7.21
Newsstand

The magazines themselves are actually standalone apps that register as Newsstand items. The difference is that many magazines and newspapers can automatically download updates or alert you with notifications when new content is available. Also note that most magazines are free to download, but to actually read any content you must subscribe or buy issues within the apps.

8

Entertain Yourself

Laptops took computing off the desk and made it more portable, but using one for enjoyable pursuits like watching movies always feels a bit like work, as if you're going to the theater and being seated in a cubicle. The keyboard is in the way, and with most laptops you find yourself scrambling to find and plug in the power cord right as something exciting is happening in the movie.

On the iPad, the movie takes over the entire device, without computer clutter getting in the way. Your music library is a few taps away. YouTube movies are ready to be streamed. AirPlay lets you watch movies on an Apple TV instantly. And Home Sharing makes it possible to play media from any computer on your network, no syncing required. As I discuss elsewhere in the book, the iPad can be incredibly productive, but it can also be a lot of fun.

Sync Media

It is odd that we use i*Tunes* as the central hub for syncing all information to the iPad, but during the early years of the iPod the only data to sync were music files. Since then, our music and movie libraries have grown alongside the capacities of Apple's players, using iTunes as the store-house for most of our digital entertainment. I've already covered the basics of syncing in Chapter 1, so in this section I'll highlight sync options that pertain specifically to music, videos, audiobooks, and podcasts.

Choose which media to sync

Depending upon the size of your iTunes media library, you may have no trouble synchronizing everything to the iPad (which is the default setting). But even if there is room, you may want to be more choosy about how you fill those bytes (so you're not stumbling over your collection of kids' music while on a business trip, for example).

1. Connect the iPad to your computer and select it in the sidebar within iTunes.

2. Click the Music tab.

3. Ensure that the Sync Music checkbox is enabled, and choose the radio button for "Selected playlists, artists, albums, and genres" (**Figure 8.1**).

4. Choose any of the following options (or ignore them and go to the next step):

    ▪ **Include music videos:** You can purchase music videos from the iTunes Store, and some albums include videos as bonus material. With this box checked, the videos are copied along with the music. If a video comes up when listening to an album, just the music plays.

- **Include voice memos:** This option is a holdover from the iPhone, which includes a Voice Memos application.

- **Automatically fill space with songs:** You bought a 64 GB iPad and don't want to waste any of that free space? This option packs the memory full of music beyond what you specify in the fields below.

Figure 8.1

Syncing music in iTunes

5. In the Playlists, Artists, Genres, and Albums lists, click checkboxes belonging to any items you wish to transfer to the iPad. Use the Search field at the top of the iTunes window to find matches quickly.

6. Click the Apply button to sync with the new options.

tip Two general sync settings that appear on the iPad summary pane in iTunes let you fit more media onto the device. "Convert higher bit rate songs to [128/192/256] kbps AAC" downsamples audio to one of three lower qualities (you choose which), reducing the songs' files sizes. "Prefer standard definition videos" leaves larger-sized HD movies on your computer and transfers only standard-definition ones.

note The "Manually manage music and videos" option lets you drag songs and video from your library to the iPad in the sidebar, which is fine if your media library isn't too large. But these days, I'd rather specify playlists than micromanage every file.

Create a Smart Playlist in iTunes

A normal playlist contains a fixed set of songs that you add manually. A *Smart* Playlist generates its content based on criteria you specify. For example, I sync a Smart Playlist that includes any media that's been added to iTunes within the last month. Here's how to build it:

1. In iTunes, choose File > New Smart Playlist.

2. Give the playlist a name.

3. From the pop-up menu, choose a selector and conditions (**Figure 8.2**).

Figure 8.2
Creating a Smart Playlist in Tunes

4. Click the + button to add more selectors, which determine what results appear. You can also nest conditions by Option-clicking (Mac) or Alt-clicking (Windows) the + button. Nesting allows you to specify that any or all of a given set of attributes is matched. For example, in addition to locating songs added in the last month, you could also specify that the genre is not Classical or Soundtrack and that the media kind is not Podcast.

5. Click OK to save the Smart Playlist.

The next time you set up your sync criteria when the iPad is connected, include that playlist. Each time you sync, the playlist is updated with new songs.

Play Music

If you're familiar with iTunes, you'll have no trouble playing music in the Music app. That said, the Music interface has a few peculiarities.

1. Tap a button at the bottom of the screen to view your library by playlist, song, artist, album, or (under More) genre, composer, podcast, or audiobook (**Figure 8.3**).

Figure 8.3
The Music interface

Library view options

2. Tap the name of a song to start playing it. The listing determines how you get to that point:

   - **Songs:** The song list is arranged alphabetically, so the songs will play back in that order.

- **Artists:** Tap an artist's name to view songs, arranged according to the albums on which they appear. If more than one album is listed, playback stops at the end of an album.

- **Albums:** Tap an album cover to view its songs, then tap a song to start playing. Albums are listed alphabetically by album title (**Figure 8.4**).

Figure 8.4
*A track list in
Albums view*

- **Genres:** Tap the icon for a genre to view albums and songs of that musical style. The songs are listed alphabetically by song title (and surprisingly, the order can't be changed unless you turn on Shuffle for playback).

- **Composers:** Tap the name of a composer to view songs he or she has composed, then tap a song to begin playing. When multiple albums appear, playback ends when the album does.

The Music app also has a Now Playing screen, which presents the song's album art, full screen; tap once anywhere to reveal the playback controls (**Figure 8.5**). In addition to offering controls for music playback and volume, the Now Playing screen includes a button in the lower-right corner to view the tracks belonging to the song's album; you can also double-tap the screen to do this. To return to Library view (without stopping playback), tap the button in the lower-left corner of the screen.

Figure 8.5
*Now Playing
screen*

Return to Library view   View album tracks

To return to the Now Playing screen at any time, tap the album art at
the top of the Library screen.

> **tip** The Now Playing screen is the only location where you can rate a song.
> Double-tap the screen to reveal album tracks and then, just above the
> track list, tap a rating (from one to five stars) for the currently playing track.

> **tip** When music is playing but the iPad's screen is locked, press the Home
> button twice to bring up a small set of playback controls.

Navigate songs

While you're listening to audio, use the following controls to skip tracks,
rewind, or fast-forward through a song (**Figure 8.6**).

Previous   Play/Pause   Next   Playhead

Figure 8.6
Playback controls

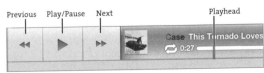

- Tap the Play/Pause button to start or stop playback.

- Tap the Previous button once to return to the beginning of the current song. Tap it twice to play the previous song in the list.

- Tap the Next button once to skip to the next song.

- Touch and hold the Previous or Next button to rewind or fast-forward through a track; holding the button longer speeds up playback.

- Drag the playhead to "scrub" to another section of a track.

tip For more control when scrubbing in the Now Playing screen, touch and hold the playhead and then drag your finger *down*. The farther down you drag, the more control you have when you then drag left or right. This feature is especially useful when moving through podcasts, audiobooks, or other lengthy tracks.

Shuffle songs

To introduce some randomness into your music listening, set your library to shuffle mode. While playing any song, tap the shuffle button (▨).

tip If you own an iPhone or iPod touch, you're probably familiar with the shake-to-shuffle feature: Simply shake the device, and the accellerometer recognizes the action and switches to shuffle play mode. The Music app on the iPad doesn't support that feature—believe me, I tried shaking, twisting, and waving my iPad and only got strange looks from the other people on the bus. My guess is that the iPad is just large enough that shaking isn't as practical when listening to music, so Apple didn't include the feature.

Repeat playback

Do you have a favorite album that begs to be repeated? In the Now Playing screen, tap the repeat button (▨) once to replay an album. Tap it again to replay the current song.

Play Genius Mixes

iTunes includes a feature called Genius Mixes, which assemble playlists based on the contents of your music library. Genius Mixes show up as playlists when you sync, and are accessible from the Playlists list in the Music app. Tap a mix to start playing it. Unlike when playing other albums, you can't see (or edit) which songs are included in a Genius Mix—you just have to trust the algorithms (which often do a pretty good job).

Listen to podcasts and audiobooks

Podcasts and audiobooks use the same playback controls as other audio tracks, but they gain a couple of extra features.

- **Change reading speed:** Since most podcasts and audiobooks are spoken-word performances, your ears are more sympathetic to other playback speeds. In the Now Playing screen, tap the speed indicator ([1x]) to the right of the scrubber bar to switch between 1x (normal), 2x (twice as fast), or ½x (half of normal).

- **Email link:** Tap the Action button (🖻) to the left of the scrubber bar to create a new outgoing message containing a link to the podcast.

- **Rewind 30 seconds:** Did you miss what someone said? Tap the 🔁 button to move the playhead back 30 seconds.

> **tip** When I'm working on my computer, I almost always have music playing. And if I need to leave, I often want to continue listening to it. A clever utility called Seamless (http://fivedetails.com/seamless/) lets me transfer the audio from the computer to my iPad or iPhone without breaking a beat.

Create Music Playlists

So far we've dealt with whatever gets sent over from the computer during a sync operation. However, the Music app is not an old-style iPod. You can build your own playlists, which get synced back the next time you connect.

Build a playlist

For a handpicked playlist, do the following:

1. Tap the New button just below the volume slider.

2. Enter a name for the playlist in the dialog that appears, and tap Save.

3. Tap the Add All Songs button to include everything listed, or tap a song's ⊕ button to add that song to the playlist. The track title becomes gray to indicate it has been included (**Figure 8.7**). You can also tap the Library view buttons, such as Artists or Albums, to choose which Music content to build from.

Figure 8.7
Building a playlist

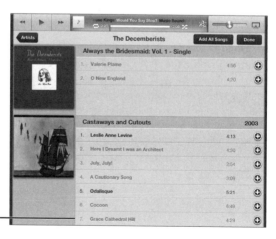

Track added
to playlist

4. Tap Done to save the playlist, which appears in the sidebar.

5. Reorder or remove the tracks if you wish, then tap the Done button.

 Tap the Edit button that appears at the top of a playlist's track listing if you want to add, delete, or rearrange songs.

Create a Genius playlist

That was quite a lot of work—what if the Music app could build a custom playlist for you? When you're listening to any song, tap the Genius button (). A set of songs based on the first one appears as a new Genius playlist (**Figure 8.8**).

Figure 8.8
A Genius playlist

Tap the Refresh button to generate a new list based on the original criteria. If you enjoyed the list, tap the Save button to turn it into a new, regular playlist.

Sync Media Using iTunes Match

Apple's iTunes Match is an interesting service: For $24.99 per year, you can download any song you own, whether you bought it from the iTunes Store, bought it from another retailer, or ripped it from a CD. What's the point if you already have that music? Let's say you bought a 16 GB iPad, and the free space is quickly going away as you add movies, photos, and other large files. You don't need to store your entire iTunes library on the iPad—just download the songs you feel like listening to.

After you sign up for the service in iTunes, the application compares your library with the database of songs offered by Apple (the "match" in iTunes Match). Anything not matched is uploaded, so even if you delete a bootleg concert recording, you can re-download it later. (The matching process can take quite a while, so I suggest you let it run overnight or longer; you'll still be able to use iTunes and play your music.)

Once you're set up with the service, go to Settings > Music on your iPad and turn on the iTunes Match option. Any music already stored on the device is erased and replaced by a listing of your full library.

note Unfortunately, iTunes Match is currently limited to 25,000 songs. If your library is larger than that, you need to trim it.

note In iTunes on a computer, you can stream that music, which is great if you own a laptop with a low-capacity solid-state drive, for example. However, on the iPad and other iOS devices, songs can only be downloaded.

Download iTunes Match tracks

To listen to your music, you must download it from iTunes using any of the following options:

- Tap the iCloud download button that appears to the right of a track (**Figure 8.9**). It is transferred to your iPad but doesn't play. (Tap the download progress indicator if you want to cancel the transfer.)

- Tap a song to begin playing and downloading it. When that song ends, the next one in the list (whether you're viewing an album, a playlist, or the full song list) automatically plays next.

- If you're viewing an album, tap Download All to receive all the tracks.

 tip The Music app can display just the items you've downloaded. Go to Settings > Music and turn the Show All Music option on or off.

Figure 8.9
*An album with
iTunes Match
enabled*

Playing   Downloading

1.	Don't Carry It All	4:17
2.	Calamity Song	3:15
3.	Rise To Me	5:00
4.	Rox In The Box	3:08
5.	January Hymn	3:13
6.	Down By The Water	3:42
7.	All Arise!	3:10

The Decemberists
The King Is Dead

Download All

Matched, not downloaded

tip Downloading your music consumes bandwidth, obviously, which you may not want to sacrifice if you own an iPad with cellular Internet service. In Settings > Music, you can turn off the Use Cellular Data option.

Upgrade low-quality songs

Having your entire music library available on any iOS device is great, but iTunes Match also has another feature that's worth its subscription price. Any track you download is formatted as a 256 kbps AAC file and isn't encumbered by digital rights management. That means you can download higher-quality files than what you may already have, at no extra cost. I wrote an article in *TidBITS* that covers the full details, including setting up Smart Playlists to find songs: http://tidbits.com/article/12872.

tip If you reach a point where your free space is starting to evaporate again, you can delete tracks by swiping across their titles and pressing the Delete button. However, that can be tedious to do on a track-by-track basis. The alternative is to nuke your music library from orbit: Go to Settings > General > Usage > Music. Swipe across the Music item and tap the Delete button that appears. All local music files are erased.

Play Videos

I love movies, but I don't get out to see them often enough. And while there are a few flicks I'd prefer to see with a large group of people, I'm happy to catch up on my movie watching at home on my own time. The iPad is great for watching a movie (or TV show, or video podcast, or movie you created) when it's most convenient.

Video sync options

Syncing video works the same as syncing music, outlined earlier in the chapter, with one helpful difference. iTunes can automatically sync items that match timely criteria, such as the five most recent unwatched movies or the three most recently added items. This option applies to any video content: movies, TV shows, and podcasts (including audio podcasts, since they're also timely items).

1. Connect the iPad and then, in iTunes, go to the Movies tab.

2. Click the checkbox for Automatically Include, and choose a range of items to copy to the iPad (**Figure 8.10**). (Of course, you can also choose not to include any movies automatically.)

Figure 8.10
Movies sync options

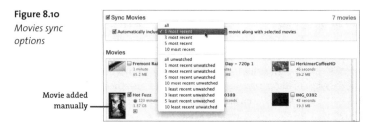

Movie added manually

3. In the Movies area that lists all available videos, click the checkbox for any item you want copied in addition to the automatic options.

You can also choose movies that appear in iTunes playlists. Mark any items in the Include Movies from Playlists area.

4. Click the Apply button to sync the iPad and copy the movies.

Watch a movie

Your content is available in the Videos app on the iPad, with different categories split among panes (Rentals, Movies, TV Shows, Podcasts, and Music Videos, depending on what's in your library) (**Figure 8.11**).

Figure 8.11
Available movies

1. Tap a video's icon to view more information about it.

2. To begin playing the movie, tap the Play button (**Figure 8.12**). Depending on the content, you can optionally tap the Chapters button to jump ahead to specific sections.

Figure 8.12
Movie info

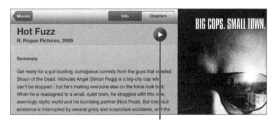

Play button

3. Sit back and enjoy the movie. If you need to interact with playback, tap the screen once to make the onscreen controls appear (**Figure 8.13**):

- Use the playback controls to play, pause, rewind, or fast-forward. They operate similarly to the music controls explained earlier, though tapping once on the Rewind or Fast-forward buttons in long movies skips the video in 5-minute increments.

- Drag the volume slider to increase or decrease the sound, or use the volume buttons on the iPad case.

- Drag the playhead to scrub through the movie.

Figure 8.13
Video controls

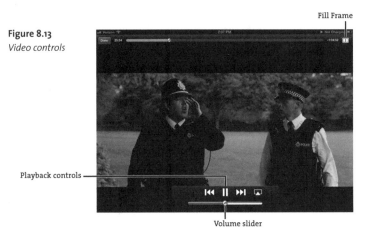

Fill Frame

Playback controls

Volume slider

- When watching widescreen movies, tap the Fill Frame button to use the entire screen (at the expense of cutting off the left and right edges of the picture).

- Some movies also include language or subtitle options, which are accessed by tapping the 🔲 button within the playback controls.

- Tap Done to return to the movie info screen.

Buy or Rent a Video

To buy or rent movies and television shows, go to the iTunes Store in iTunes on your computer or tap the iTunes app on your iPad. Searching for and purchasing videos is similar to buying other things from the iTunes storefronts, but with a few annoying restrictions.

- The iPad can play HD movies, but some titles can only be purchased in SD (standard definition), some can be rented or purchased in SD, and some can be rented in HD only on the iPad. This crazy and confusing distinction is the result of the movies' rights holders (Hollywood studios) trying to wring profit, establish some measure of misguided control, or...well, to be honest I don't know. What's worse is that the availability of these options changes over time; some movies previously available for rent can only be purchased, or no longer appear in the iTunes Store. What this means for you and me is that we need to make sure we examine what we're about to purchase or rent.

- HD movies you rented on the iPad can be viewed only on the iPad, not transferred to your computer or another device. HD movies you rent in iTunes on your computer can be transferred to the iPad—but sometimes the HD version is available only on the iPad. (However, AirPlay helps in this regard, as I'll discuss shortly.)

- After renting a movie, you must watch it within 30 days. If you don't, the movie is automatically deleted from your library.

- Once you begin to watch a rental, you must finish watching it within 24 hours, at which point it's deleted.

note   I apologize for sounding cranky, but I should be able to purchase a movie—in SD or HD, if available—and watch it wherever I want, especially if it's within Apple's ecosystem. As it is, Apple and the studios are making it difficult for people like me to give them money that I'm willing to part with in exchange for entertainment, which is a terrible business model.

Download previously purchased videos

Apple uses your Apple ID to remember everything you've purchased from the iTunes Store. It's a bit of accounting that doesn't come as a surprise, except for one thing: You can re-download almost anything you've purchased. (I say "almost" because, as of this writing, not all studios are authorizing this capability.)

1. On the iPad, open the iTunes app.

2. Tap the Purchased button at the bottom of the screen.

3. Tap the View button to choose which media to list: songs, TV shows, or movies.

4. Locate the item you want to download and tap the iCloud download button.

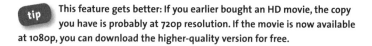 **This feature gets better:** If you earlier bought an HD movie, the copy you have is probably at 720p resolution. If the movie is now available at 1080p, you can download the higher-quality version for free.

Watch Your Own Movies

The iTunes Store isn't the only source of movies, of course. Home movies you shoot and edit can be viewed on the iPad, too. Export them from your video editing software (such as iMovie or Windows Live Movie Maker) to iTunes as .m4v, .mp4, or .mov files. Once in iTunes, movies can be synced to the iPad.

Convert DVDs

What about movies you already own on DVD? Using software such as HandBrake (www.handbrake.fr), you can convert a movie to a digital file that can be imported into iTunes and synced to the iPad. This option is great if you're going on a long trip and don't want to bring along a stack of plastic discs, or for storing kids' entertainment when you don't want the original disc to be damaged. (The iPad is already a favorite for kids and parents on lengthy car or plane trips.)

note It's worth pointing out here that I'm not a lawyer, and that the practice of encoding DVDs is technically against the law in the United States due to the Digital Millennium Copyright Act (DMCA). Making digital copies of movies you've legally purchased seems like a legitimate fair use to me, and is far preferable to downloading questionably ripped movies from the Internet. The Electronic Frontier Foundation provides more information about the topic (www.eff.org/issues/drm).

Stream Media

The iPad is a wireless device, yet you need to connect it to a computer to sync movies and other entertainment to it over the USB cable. Or do you? A few wireless options truly let you watch video almost anywhere.

AirPlay

I've watched quite a few movies and TV shows on the iPad, but sometimes I want to watch something on a much bigger screen. If you have a second- or third-generation Apple TV (the small, black unit), you can play a video directly between the iPad and the Apple TV by tapping one button. AirPlay also works for playing music to the Apple TV or to an AirPort Express connected to a stereo.

If an Apple TV or AirPort Express is on the same Wi-Fi network as your iPad, an AirPlay button appears near the playback controls.

1. Begin playing a video or song. This feature isn't limited to just the Videos and Music apps; most apps that can display media, such as Safari, can play media on other devices using AirPlay.

2. Tap the AirPlay button (**Figure 8.14**).

Figure 8.14
Choosing an AirPlay source in the Videos app

AirPlay button

3. Choose an AirPlay device from the list that appears. After a few seconds, for video, the picture disappears from the iPad and starts playing on the television, right where you left off; for both video and audio, the AirPlay button turns blue to indicate it's active.

4. When you want to resume playing the media on your iPad, tap the button and choose iPad from the popover.

Home Sharing

Over the years, I've accumulated movies, TV shows, and music that now reside on a large hard drive attached to a computer at home. In the past, syncing files to watch was a hassle, but now I can access it all through Apple's Home Sharing feature. Specify your Apple ID on the iPad to stream content from computers on your network.

 You need to set the same Apple ID for all devices on your network that will use Home Sharing.

Set up Home Sharing

The setting to enable Home Sharing on the iPad is a little hidden:

1. Open Settings > Music.

2. Under Home Sharing, enter your Apple ID and password.

3. Tap Done on the onscreen keyboard.

Play media stored on another machine

To play media via Home Sharing, do the following:

1. Open the Music or Videos app (depending on what you want to play).

2. In Music, tap the More button (**Figure 8.15**); in Videos, tap the Shared button at the top of the screen.

Figure 8.15
*Selecting a
library using
Home Sharing*

3. Tap the name of the shared library you want to access.

4. Locate the media you want to play, just as if the content were stored on your iPad.

5. If you want to disconnect from the computer, tap the name of the active library in Music or return to the main screen in Videos.

tip Another option for home streaming is to run an app such as AirVideo or StreamToMe. These apps don't require an Apple ID, and you can specify media sources (such as additional folders) outside iTunes.

Streaming-video services

Members of the movie rental service Netflix can download the free Netflix app for the iPad and take advantage of the company's growing library of Watch Now titles.

Other popular options are the ABC Player app and the PBS for iPad app, which provide streaming versions of the networks' programs. (ABC does not allow streaming over a cellular connection, however.) Episodes are typically available the day after they air on broadcast television. As another example, Hulu Plus members can download a free app to watch other TV programs.

Play Videos on a Television Using Cables

AirPlay over a wireless network isn't the only option for playing videos on the TV. There are four options, depending on the TV's connectors: the Digital AV Adapter (HDMI), the Component AV Cable Kit, the Composite AV Cable Kit, and the iPad Dock Connector to VGA Adapter. The HDMI adapter and the component kit have the advantage of being digital, versus analog, so they enable you to play protected content (such as videos bought from the iTunes Store).

Although the iPad can play back 1080p HD video, some of the kits don't offer it. The component kit offers 576p (usually 720 by 576 pixels) and 480p (usually 640 by 480); the composite kit handles 576i and 480i (the same resolutions, but interlaced instead of progressive-scan). The HDMI adapter can do 1080p from the iPad.

9

Find Yourself with Maps

If anything about the iPad makes me feel like I'm living in the future (well, there are a lot of things), it's the Maps app. Within a few seconds, I can look up an address, find a nearby business, go virtual sightseeing with my daughter, or get directions from my current location—wherever that happens to be—to any address.

The Maps app uses Google's mapping technology to deliver results that can be a typical street map or a top-down satellite view that really does feel like science fiction. As long as you have an Internet connection, you can find yourself. As someone who's never had a good sense of direction, that's incredible.

The iPad Wi-Fi + 4G model includes a GPS chip for accurate location discovery, but the Wi-Fi–only model can also use Maps well.

Find Yourself

For a quick taste of what the Maps app can do, launch it and tap the Current Location (🥅) button. The first time you do this, Maps asks for your permission to use your location.

The map zooms in, indicating your location with a blue sphere (**Figure 9.1**). The pale circle emanating from the sphere represents how accurate the location is: A large circle means you're located somewhere within that area. If you see no circle (other than a faint pulse to make the sphere more visible), it means the iPad has pinpointed its location.

Figure 9.1
Finding location in Maps

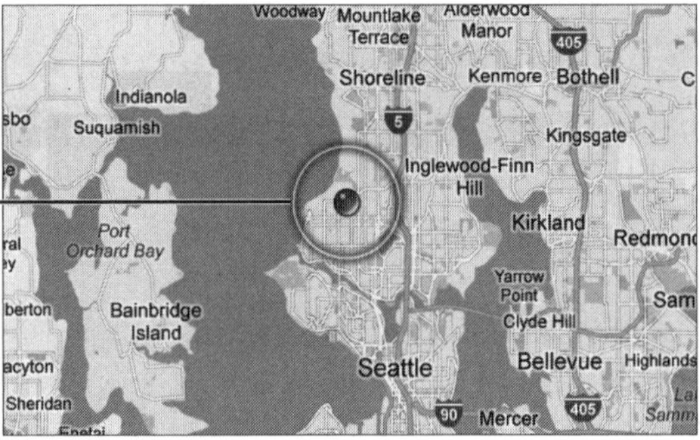

Neato movie-style visual pulsing effect marking exact location

To navigate the map, do any of the following:

- Drag with one finger to reposition the map. As you move around, the map redraws areas previously outside the borders of the frame. At any time you can tap the Current Location button to re-center the map on your position.

- Pinch two fingers to zoom in or out. You can pinch and move at the same time, too.

- Double-tap anywhere on the screen to zoom in on that area.

- Both iPad models include a compass, a chip that can determine which direction it's pointed. Tap the Current Location button again to orient the view according to the direction you're facing (**Figure 9.2**).

Figure 9.2
Compass view

Compass points north.

Fan indicates the direction you're facing.

> **tip** The compass works best when the iPad is held flat, parallel to the ground. You may need to recalibrate it occasionally by (I'm not kidding) waving the iPad in a figure-eight motion in the air.

Location Services: How the iPad Knows Position

The iPad with 4G includes a chip that picks up GPS (Global Positioning Satellite) signals and translates them into an accurate physical location. The Wi-Fi–only model does not contain a GPS chip, but Maps still works. How?

Apple designed a system it calls Location Services, which takes GPS and cellular location data (if available) to come up with an accurate fix on your position. It's possible to reset Location Services (in case you accidentally tapped Don't Allow for an app), although it clears all permissions; you'll need to grant access to apps again the next time they ask. Go to Settings > General > Reset, and tap the Reset Location Warnings button. You can also disable Location Services in Settings > General or turn it off for specific apps.

Map views

The Maps app offers four map views that cater to people who find routes in different ways. If you feel turned around using the Standard style, you may find it helpful to see landmarks in Satellite view, for instance. To access the other styles, tap the page curl at the lower-right corner of the screen (**Figure 9.3**). Tap a style to switch to it (**Figure 9.4**).

Figure 9.3
Tapping the page curl to reveal Maps settings

Page curl —

Figure 9.4
A composite of the map styles

Standard   Terrain

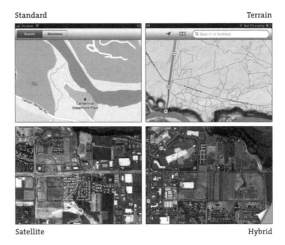

Satellite   Hybrid

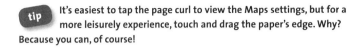

tip It's easiest to tap the page curl to view the Maps settings, but for a more leisurely experience, touch and drag the paper's edge. Why? Because you can, of course!

Find Locations

Now that you know where you are, it's time to go exploring. The Search field can accept nearly any query, not just addresses. Type "coffee," for example, and results appear as red pins on the map. You can also start typing a specific company name, the name of a person or company in your Contacts list, or the name of an earlier search result.

Tap a pin to identify the location (**Figure 9.5**). If you don't see what you're looking for, the match may be outside the current screen view. Tap the ⊜ button in the Search field to display a popover containing all the results.

Figure 9.5
Search results as pins

Locations —

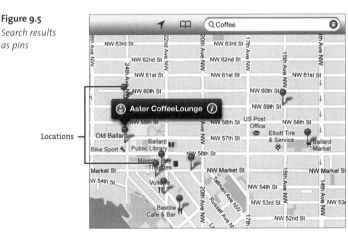

Get information about a location

To learn more about a location, tap the 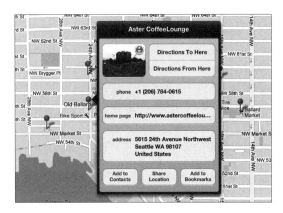 button. The label expands to display more information and options (**Figure 9.6**).

Figure 9.6
More information about a location

- Tap the Home Page label to visit the site in Safari.

- Tap the Add to Contacts button to create a new contact record containing all of the information.

- Tap the Share Location button to compose an email message containing a URL to view the location on Google Maps and the location as a vCard file (for easy import into most address book applications).

- Tap Add to Bookmarks to save the location for the future. It will be available by tapping the Bookmarks button in the toolbar.

- Tap one of the Directions buttons to view a route to the location; see "Get Directions," coming up in this chapter.

- Touch and hold any field, and then tap the Copy option that appears to copy just that information for pasting elsewhere (such as in an outgoing email message).

Visit Street View

If you see a Street View icon () on a location's label, tap it to see what the place looks like if you're standing in front of it. I like this feature a lot, because I can better see what a building looks like so I don't miss it (**Figure 9.7**).

Figure 9.7
Street View

Intended location

Tap to navigate
down the street.

Tap to exit
Street View.

tip Double-tap or pinch within the Street View mode to zoom in. Tap once again to view the address larger at the top of the screen, as well as a Report button that can be used to report inappropriate content captured by the Street View cameras.

note Consider Street View images a rough reference, because often something will have changed—a building repainted, a tree removed—in the time since the photo was taken.

Drop a pin

In addition to finding locations through a search, you can drop a pin on an arbitrary location to get a little more information about it or to mark a spot for reference.

1. Touch and hold an area of the screen. A purple pin lands there, with the address of the location listed in its label (**Figure 9.8**).

Figure 9.8
Dropped pin

2. Touch and hold the pin to lift it from the map, and then drag it to a more specific location if you want.

   Tapping the *i* icon reveals the options for copying and saving the address. If Street View is available for that location, tap the Street View button to see the location.

 A more laborious way to drop a pin is to tap the page curl to reveal the Maps settings and then tap the Drop Pin button.

To remove a pin, tap the *i* icon and then tap the Remove Pin button.

If you touch and hold the screen to drop a new pin, the previous one disappears. You can have only one purple pin on the map at one time.

Get Directions

I used to think that getting and printing directions from a mapping service on my computer was pretty cool, but now I don't even bother with the paper. It's easy to get directions between two locations in the Maps app—and not just driving directions, but walking and bus routes, too (where that information is available).

1. Tap the Directions button in the upper-left corner to switch to
   Directions mode. The Search field splits into two fields: the starting
   point and the destination. The iPad assumes you want to start at your
   current location, but you can search for others.

2. Enter a destination by doing a search in the second field (**Figure 9.9**).

Figure 9.9
Searching for
a destination

To change the starting point, tap the first field and enter a search term
or address. If you had previously dropped a pin, you can select its location by tapping the first field and selecting the address in purple text.

 **If you're viewing information about an address, tap the Directions
From Here or Directions To Here button to initiate a search.**

3. Tap Search on the onscreen keyboard to reveal the route, which appears
   as a blue line between the two points (**Figure 9.10**). For easier identification, the starting point is a green pin and the destination is a red pin.

Figure 9.10
Destination,
known

Route —

4. If multiple routes are offered, tap one to choose it.

5. Driving is the default mode of transport, but you don't need to be car-centric. Using the directions bar at the bottom of the screen, tap an icon to reveal the bus route or walking directions.

The bus route is particularly helpful. Tap the clock icon on the directions bar to look up schedules and connections; you can also tap a bus stop to view the route number and departure time (**Figure 9.11**).

Figure 9.11
Bus route information

Follow the directions

As you travel, the Maps app can give you step-by-step directions (presumably so someone in the passenger seat can guide you if you're driving; be safe out there, kids).

1. Tap the Start button in the directions bar.

2. Tap the arrow buttons to go to the next or previous step in the route. The bar lists directions for each step, and the route indicates where you are and where you've been (**Figure 9.12**). If you prefer a text list of directions, tap the button at the left of the bar.

Figure 9.12
A trip in progress

Tap to reveal
text directions.

3. Continue tapping the arrow button until you've reached the
   destination.

tip   When it's time to head home, tap the curved-arrow button ([S])
between the search fields to swap the starting point and the
destination.

Step-by-Step vs. Turn-by-Turn

The directions in the Maps app don't advance automatically, the way
some GPS devices do. Those offer turn-by-turn directions, where the
device plots your course and tells you, audibly, when to make the
next turn. The GPS chip inside the 4G iPad enables that same functionality using some third-party software, such as CoPilot Live HD
North America.

10

Be Productive

The iPad isn't Apple's first foray into producing a PDA, or "personal digital assistant." The company created the category—and coined the term, even—with the Newton handheld. But the Newton wasn't adopted as broadly as its upstart competitor the PalmPilot, and when Steve Jobs returned to Apple in 1997, he killed the Newton. As Palm ascended and Windows Mobile devices appeared (and disappeared), people wondered when Apple would get back into the game. I think rumors of a new Apple PDA started floating around the day the Newton died.

A decade later, Apple finally created its modern PDA: the iPhone. Yes, it was a phone, but the phone aspect was just a way to put it into a familiar category. The iPhone, and now the iPad on a grander scale, is capable of storing and making accessible all of your personal information: your schedule, list of contacts, notes, snippets, ideas, and doodles.

Sync Personal Information

Although it's possible to create new events, contacts, and notes on the iPad (detailed in this chapter), most of that information probably already exists on your computer. There are two ways of transferring it to the iPad and keeping it updated: syncing wirelessly using iCloud, Google, Yahoo, or Microsoft Exchange; or through iTunes over the dock connector cable.

iCloud, Google, or Yahoo wireless sync

The ability to synchronize personal information wirelessly is one of my favorite features of iCloud (formerly MobileMe). If I edit an event on my computer, the change is propagated to my iPad, iPhone, and other computers within a minute or so. Wireless syncing with iCloud, Google, or Yahoo must be set up on the iPad, not in iTunes.

1. Go to Settings > Mail, Contacts, Calendars and tap the Add Account button.

2. Tap the button for your provider.

3. Enter your name, email address, and password. Tap Next.

4. Enable the services you want to sync (**Figure 10.1**), and tap the Save button. After a few minutes, your data transfers to the iPad. (These options are also available in the iCloud settings for your primary iCloud account.)

Figure 10.1
Setting up iCloud on the iPad

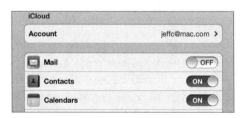

iCloud

| Account | jeffc@mac.com > |

Mail	OFF
Contacts	ON
Calendars	ON

tip It's possible to sync via iCloud and via iTunes. For example, you may want to sync your calendars via iCloud but store only business contacts on the iPad. In that case you'd turn off the Contacts sync option for iCloud and enable specific contact groups in the Info pane in iTunes.

tip Regardless of your sync method, you probably don't want every event in the past to appear on your calendar. Go to Settings > Mail, Contacts, Calendars, scroll down to the Calendars section, tap the Sync button, and specify a time period (such as Events 3 Months Back) of events to include during a sync.

Exchange sync

If your company manages its email, contacts, and calendars using Microsoft Exchange, you can tie the iPad into the system with little fuss.

1. Go to Settings > Mail, Contacts, Calendars and tap Add Account.

2. Tap the Microsoft Exchange button.

3. Enter your email address, username, and password. Tap Next.

4. After the information is verified, tap Next again.

5. Enable the services you want to sync (mail, contacts, and calendars), and tap the Save button. After a few minutes, the data transfers.

iTunes sync

iTunes is the gateway between your data and the iPad, whether the data happens to be your music library or your schedule. With the iPad connected, do the following:

1. Select the iPad in the sidebar and click the Info button. You'll find categories for contacts, calendars, "other" (notes and bookmarks), and mail accounts. (For details on mail accounts, see Chapter 4.)

2. Click the category checkboxes to enable syncing those items (**Figure 10.2**). Under Mac OS X, contacts and calendars are synced with Address Book and iCal (or, more specifically, with the underlying databases that those applications access). Under Windows, choose the data source from the pop-up menu in the category name; contacts, for example, can sync with Windows Contacts, Google Contacts, or Yahoo Address Book by default.

Figure 10.2

Syncing info in iTunes

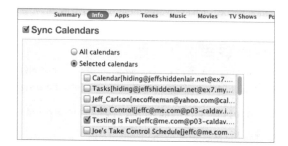

3. Within each category, choose to sync all items or selected ones.

4. Click the Apply button to make the changes and sync the iPad.

Manage Your Schedule

Some people live and die by their calendars, while others refer to their schedules only occasionally. The Calendar app fits both personalities.

View your calendar

When you open the Calendar app, your schedule appears in one of four views, all evoking the look of a paper-and-leather desk calendar. Tap a view button at the top of the screen.

Each view has its own focus—the Day view, for example, shows a schedule of the day on the right-hand page, with a small red pin indicating the current time. The day's events are listed at left (**Figure 10.3**).

Figure 10.3
Calendar
Day view

Event
(in list and
in schedule)

Current time

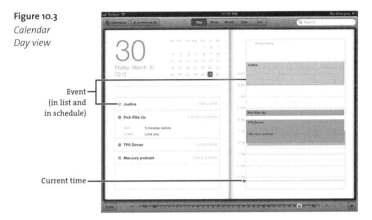

Choose from a variety of ways to switch between dates:

■ Swipe left or right to view next or previous dates.

■ Tap the Today button to jump to today's date in any view.

■ Tap the triangular buttons on either side of the timeline below the calendar to switch to the previous or next item. Tapping in the Week view, for instance, shifts to the next week.

■ Tap a block of time on the timeline to jump directly to it (**Figure 10.4**).

Figure 10.4
Navigation bar

Previous button

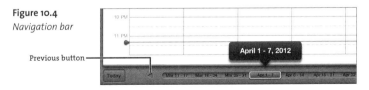

tip Touch and drag on the timeline to rapidly skim forward or backward in time. If you hold at the edge, the pop-up display indicates how far you're traveling. Lift your finger to then display that date. This trick has some subtlety to it, too: After you've reached the edge, drag past it to make the dates fly by faster; drag your finger back to the edge to slow it down.

- In the Day view, tap a date in the calendar grid to jump to it.

- In the Month view, double-tap a date to switch to the Day view.

- Type a term into the Search box and tap the Search key on the onscreen keyboard. Touch any event in the Results popover to jump to it.

tip The Results popover that appears begins to find matches as you type, but I've found that it doesn't catch everything; you need to tap the Search key to perform a thorough search.

Create or edit an event

A common scenario in my kitchen: While we're making dinner, my wife and I talk about what's happening during the week, specifically events our daughter attends. I often reach for the iPad to view the week, add new events, or edit current ones that have changed. I don't need to go upstairs to my computer to do that. And when I do get to my desk later, the changes are already applied, thanks to wireless syncing.

The following steps illustrate how to create a new event, but the steps are almost identical for editing existing events.

1. To create a new event, do one of the following:

   - Tap the + button in the lower-right corner. The Add Event popover appears.

   - Touch and hold at the day or time you want the event to occur. Without lifting your finger, you can drag the event to a specific time.

2. Type a name for the event in the Title field. You can also optionally add a location (**Figure 10.5**).

Figure 10.5
Adding a title and location

3. Tap the Starts/Ends field and, using the dials below, set a starting date and time and then an ending date and time (**Figure 10.6**). If the event doesn't have a specific time, enable the All-day option. Tap Done.

Figure 10.6
The slot-machine scheduler

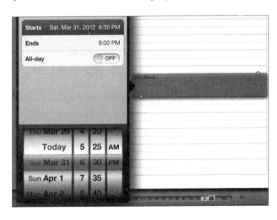

You can also grab the top and bottom handles of the event to adjust the start and end times, or you can drag the event to a new time.

4. If the event is recurring, tap the Repeat button and specify how often: Every Day, Every Week, Every 2 Weeks, Every Month, or Every Year. Tap Done to return to the previous screen.

5. Tap the Alert button if you want an alarm to go off before the event, and then specify a time. Tap Done.

6. Choose which of your synced calendars the event will appear in. (You can specify a default calendar in Settings > Mail, Contacts, Calendars.)

7. Enter any miscellaneous details in the Notes field.

8. Tap Done.

Editing an existing event initially depends on which view you're in. Do one of the following, then use the previous steps to alter the information:

- In the Day view, tap it once.

- To edit in the Week and Month views, tap an event once and then tap the Edit button that appears (**Figure 10.7**).

- For the List view, tap an event to select it, then tap it again to bring up the editing popover.

Figure 10.7
Editing in Week view

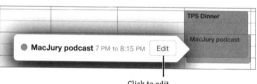

Click to edit.

Reply to an event invitation

When someone invites you to an event using a calendar service that supports the feature (such as Exchange or iCloud), the event appears in the Calendar app as a new invitation.

1. Open the Calendar app and tap the event, which appears with a dotted outline (**Figure 10.8**). You can also tap the Invitations button at the top of the screen to view a list of invitations.

2. Tap Accept, Decline, or Maybe to reply to the invitation.

Figure 10.8
Incoming invitation

You can change your reply later by viewing details about the event and tapping one of the reply buttons.

Hide or show calendars

The Calendar app tries hard to appear like a paper desk calendar, but here's one area where paper just wouldn't cut it. To juggle several kinds of events—business, personal, kids' schedules, and so on—you'd need separate physical calendars (or a handful of colored pens). Here you can include digital calendars for each category, color-code them, and show or hide them as you please.

New calendars must be created in your desktop software and synced to the iPad. Once there, in the Calendar app, tap the Calendars button and tap the ones you wish to hide (the checkmark disappears) (**Figure 10.9**). The events are still there, but they aren't cluttering up your calendar views.

Figure 10.9
Choosing calendars to show

Manage Your Contacts

Over the years, my list of contacts has grown in size to the point where I know some of the information is out of date, but I don't have the time or desire to clean it all up. And really, I don't need to. The Contacts app stores it all for me so I can easily find a person's essential information.

Contacts also ties in to many other areas of the iPad, feeding email addresses for Mail and physical addresses for Maps. When you start typing someone's name in an outgoing email message, you're matching a record in the Contacts app—so you don't have to remember that your cousin Jeremy's address is actually b4conlov3r42lol@aol.com.

Find a contact

The Contacts app maintains the same spirit of the Calendar app, presenting your contacts in an address book (**Figure 10.10**). Flick through the list to browse for a contact, or use the tabs to advance through the alphabet.

Figure 10.10
The Contacts address book

Drag your finger down tabs to jump to contacts.

Tap a name to view its details.

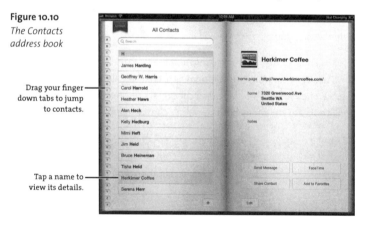

tip Contacts are listed in order of their last names, but you can change this preference. Go to Settings > Mail, Contacts, Calendars, tap Sort Order in the Contacts section, and change the option to "First, Last." The Display Order option in the same section dictates how each line appears (for example, changing that option to "Last, First" would make my name appear as Carlson Jeff). In either case, the last name appears in bold for easier identification.

If you know the name of the person or company you're trying to find (or even part of the name, or a detail that might be in their information), tap the Search field and begin typing. Results appear immediately, with the first one displayed at right (**Figure 10.11**).

Figure 10.11
Find a contact.

Normally, all contacts are listed, but if you've organized your contacts in groups on your computer, you can display just the contacts from a group.

1. Tap the Groups button at upper left, which looks like a red bookmark.

2. In the list of groups, tap the one you want to focus on. The page turns back to the contacts list, showing only that group's members.

note Although you can view groups on the iPad, the Contacts app offers no way to create new groups or move a person to a new group. You'll need to do that in your desktop software and then sync the changes to the iPad.

Create or edit a contact

I've learned the hard way that I possess a superhuman ability to repel important scraps of paper. Rather than jot down someone's contact information on the edge of an envelope, I prefer to add their details to the Contacts app so I know it won't get lost.

 tip Before you begin: If you want a new contact to belong to one of your groups, first make sure that group is the one selected.

1. Tap the New Contact button (+) to create a new record, or tap the Edit button to change details of an existing record.

2. Tap each relevant field and type the person's contact information (**Figure 10.12**).

Figure 10.12
*Entering
information for a
new contact*

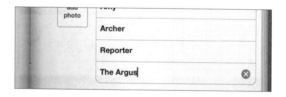

3. A contact can contain multiple similar items, such as phone numbers. As soon as you start entering information in one field, the Contacts app automatically adds another one below it, anticipating that you may want to add, for instance, a work number and then a home number. To remove any fields already made, tap the red Delete button.

   If you don't see a field you're looking for, such as Job Title, scroll to the bottom of the list, tap Add Field, and choose from the options.

4. For fields with labels (such as Home, Work, or Mobile), tap the current label to view a popover containing alternates. If the one you want isn't listed, choose Add Custom Label and type your own.

5. To add a photo to the contact, tap the Add Photo box, which presents two options:

   - **Take Photo.** The camera interface opens, allowing you to take a picture either of yourself or of someone on the other side of the rear-facing camera. Tap the shutter button to capture the shot, move and scale it to fit, and tap the Use button.

   - **Choose Photo.** Locate and tap an image in your photo albums. Position it in the frame as you'd like it to appear, and then tap the Use button (**Figure 10.13**).

6. Tap Done when you're finished creating the contact. You can change details later by tapping the Edit button.

Figure 10.13
Grab an image from your Photos library.

tip If you haven't done so yet, be sure to create a record for yourself. Safari uses that information for its AutoFill feature (go to Settings > Safari > AutoFill, tap My Info, and specify your entry). It's also good for sharing your details with someone else.

Share a contact

Early handhelds from Palm included an infrared receiver that would let two Palm-wielding people "beam" contact information to each other. Not only was it incredibly geeky, it was extremely useful. In just a few seconds, one person's full contact information was in the other's contacts list. That was before devices were networked; now, we just bounce the same information out to the Internet and into someone's email inbox. To share a record from your Contacts list, do the following:

1. Locate the contact within the list and open it.

2. Tap the Share Contact button, and choose whether to send an email or a text message. A new outgoing email or text message appears, containing a vCard file attachment that can be imported into most contact software.

3. Enter the address of the person who will receive the contact.

4. Tap the Send button.

Receive a shared contact

If you're on the receiving end of a shared contact, you can easily add someone's vCard to the Contacts list.

1. In the Mail app, locate the email message that includes the .vcf file attachment.

2. Tap the attachment to view the contact information (**Figure 10.14**).

3. Tap either the Create New Content button or the Add to Existing Contact button to transfer the information to the Contacts app.

Figure 10.14
*Adding a contact
from email*

Delete a contact

If you find yourself standing in line somewhere with nothing to do and suddenly feel the urge to purge old records from your Contacts list, do the following:

1. Tap a contact name to view it.

2. Tap the Edit button.

3. Scroll to the bottom of the information and tap the Delete Contact button.

4. In the confirmation dialog that appears, tap the Delete button. That contact is removed from the list. (Unfortunately, Contacts does not support the near-universal shortcut of swiping across a record to delete it.)

Take Notes

Let's see, the iPad is roughly the size of a pad of paper, easy to hold in the hand, and capable of storing a lot of information. When you need to jot down some ideas, the Notes app is ready with a familiar yellow legal pad (mounted in a virtual leather holder, even, when viewed in landscape orientation).

Create a note

Here comes the hard part. Tap the New Note button (■) and start typing. (Actually, not so hard.)

The first line of the note becomes the title, which appears in the toolbar and in the Notes list. In landscape orientation, that list sits off to the side (**Figure 10.15**); in portrait mode, tap the Notes button to bring up a popover containing all the notes you've stored.

Figure 10.15
The Notes app, viewed wide

Notes list —

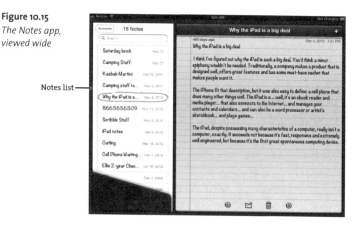

If you're looking for something in particular, enter a term in the Search field at the top of the Notes list (**Figure 10.16**).

Figure 10.16
*Searching notes,
viewed tall*

Search field

Edit a note

Tap a note in the list to view it. You can also tap the Previous and Next buttons at the bottom of the page to switch between notes (**Figure 10.17**).

Figure 10.17
*Notes controls,
with my own
homemade labels*

To edit, tap somewhere on the note to place the cursor, and start typing.

Delete a note

There are two ways to delete a note:

- With the note visible, tap the Trash button, then tap the Delete Note button.
- In the Notes list, swipe one finger across a note's title and tap the Delete button that appears.

tip If the handwriting-style font in Notes isn't your style, go to Settings > Notes and choose Helvetica as the typeface.

Sync notes

We've already covered the mechanics of setting up the iPad to sync notes—it's a checkbox in the Info pane in iTunes, or, for wireless sync, a setting under Mail, Contacts, Calendars. But where do the notes go on your computer? On the Mac, they show up in the Mail application. Under Windows, you need Microsoft Outlook 2003, 2007, or later.

Share notes

Tap the Mail icon at the bottom of the note to send its contents in an outgoing email message or to print the note.

tip A lot of alternative note-taking apps for the iPad are available at the App Store. I bounce between Simplenote (simple-note.appspot.com) and PlainText (www.hogbaysoftware.com), which feature clean interfaces for writing notes and the ability to sync to Dropbox. For more bells and whistles, check out Evernote (www.evernote.com), a catch-all app and Web service that can store text, images, and audio for later. If you prefer writing notes by hand, try Paper (www.fiftythree.com) or other drawing apps, and consider buying a stylus such as the Cosmonaut (www.studioneat.com).

tip If you find yourself doing a lot of typing on the iPad—or if you're taking it along on a trip instead of a laptop—I highly recommend the Apple Wireless Keyboard. Other Bluetooth keyboards also work; although I haven't used it, colleagues rave about the ZAGGfolio (www.zagg.com), which is a Bluetooth keyboard integrated with a case. Another possibility, if you want to use a physical keyboard, is to purchase the iPad Camera Connection Kit and use the USB adapter to connect a USB keyboard. (Some keyboards require more power than the iPad can provide, in which case you need to connect the keyboard through a powered USB hub.)

Set Up Reminders

Until iOS 5, the iPad, iPhone, and iPod touch didn't offer a to-do list app. It was a curious omission, filled quickly by many developers with apps such as OmniFocus (www.omnigroup.com) and Wunderlist (www.wunderlist.com). Apple finally joined the party with Reminders, a simple to-do app that syncs to iCloud.

To create a new reminder, do the following:

1. In the Reminders app, tap the New button (+).

2. Type the title of the reminder and then tap Return on the keyboard.

3. Tap the task name to edit or add details, such as its priority and notes (**Figure 10.18**). You can also tap Remind Me to display a notification at a certain date and time or assign the task to another Reminders list. (Some options are available after tapping the Show More button.)

4. Tap Done to finish.

Figure 10.18
Editing a reminder

tip Tap the Edit button at the top of the screen to create new lists, delete existing ones, or rearrange the list order. Unfortunately, you can't reorder the reminders themselves.

note If you also use Reminders on an iPhone, you'll find some options missing on the iPad, such as displaying a reminder when you arrive at a geographic location or being able to dictate a new reminder by voice (which requires Siri).

Move Data Files to and from the iPad

The iPad envisions a future where people don't need to worry about file management. Using the Finder under Mac OS X, or Windows Explorer on a PC, leads to all sorts of gunk under the hood: *Where are my documents? If the desktop is right there behind my windows, why is it also a folder? Why can't I find the file I just saved?* We've coped with it for years because that was just the way it was. According to Apple's view of the world, an iPad owner shouldn't be exposed to all that. You create something. It's just there. End of story.

But we're not quite there yet. Like it or not, we still have to deal with files, and right now the process of getting them on and off the iPad is a bit of a mess.

There are currently three ways of transferring files that can be opened by applications on the iPad: send them via email, use iTunes as the gateway, or use a network service such as iCloud, Dropbox, or SugarSync.

Use email

Because the Mail app recognizes many common file types, you can send an email to yourself, receive the message on the iPad, and view the attachment. See Chapter 4 for more details.

Copy to the Apps pane

Apps that can accept outside files appear at the bottom of the Apps pane in iTunes (**Figure 10.19**).

Figure 10.19
*Sharing files
in iTunes*

Files on the iPad

1. Click the iPad app that you want to use to open your file.

2. Click the Add button and locate the file you want to transfer. Or, drag the file from the desktop to the Documents pane. The file is trans-ferred immediately; you don't have to sync the iPad.

3. On the iPad, launch the app and use it to open the file.

To get documents back out, reverse the process: Connect to iTunes, and in the Apps pane, select an app, select the file you want, and either drag it to the desktop or click the Save To button and specify a destination.

> **tip** Wait, you thought it would be that easy? Depending on the app, you may need to take an extra step. In Apple's iWork apps, you must export the file first to place it in a directory that is accessible to iTunes. Other apps may have a better option; be sure to check their documentation.

Sync with iCloud or another network service

The other way to transfer files is via the Internet, using a service such as iCloud, Dropbox (www.dropbox.com), or SugarSync (www.sugarsync.com). Files stored on the iPad are synchronized with a network server, which you can then access using your computer without needing to plug in a cable.

Alas, that route is also still somewhat muddled, despite the obvious advantage it would present. iCloud has a noble goal: that your file just be available from wherever you connect to iCloud. Currently, as you work on a document in Pages on the iPad, for example, all changes are automatically saved to iCloud. Open Pages on an iPhone and pick up where you left off.

On the Mac, though, it's still not so smooth as I write this. You can send files to iWork.com, but it's not a direct process. First you must share the file to iWork.com, which sends the file via email instead of transferring it directly. To get the file onto your computer, you visit iWork.com, download the file, and *then* open it in an iWork app. I anticipate that direct iCloud support will arrive in the next version of iWork on the Mac, but it hasn't happened yet.

A better solution for now is synchronization to services like Dropbox and SugarSync. They sync the contents of folders on your computer and make them available on the iPad, where you can preview them or open them in supported apps. Some apps, such as PlainText, save files directly to Dropbox, making them available on other devices and computers immediately.

11

Be Secure

Most of the best qualities of the iPad can also be liabilities. It's portable, so you're more likely to take it with you to a coffee shop or to class, where there's greater chance of losing it or having it stolen. Being out "in the wild" also increases the chance that the wireless network you connect to—or even someone at the next table—is scanning for sensitive data like credit card numbers. The iPad stores your personal digital information, so a thief would have access to your contact information.

Security isn't all cloak-and-dagger stuff, though. If you're sharing an iPad among your family, you may not want the kids to get online and download all of their favorite albums from the iTunes Store—on your credit card. With some reasonable precautions, you can make your iPad experience more secure.

Set a Passcode to Unlock

The easiest front-line measure you can take to improve the iPad's security is to set a passcode lock that must be entered when the iPad is woken from sleep. The passcode can be a four-digit number or a longer, more secure phrase (**Figure 11.1**).

Figure 11.1
Unlocking the iPad using a phrase

1. Go to Settings > General and tap the Passcode Lock button.

2. To require an alphanumeric passcode, turn the Simple Passcode switch to Off. Otherwise, proceed to the next step to use a four-digit number.

3. Tap the Turn Passcode On button, which brings up the Set Passcode dialog (**Figure 11.2**).

4. Enter a four-digit code, then re-enter it to confirm.

5. The passcode dialog is initially set to appear whenever you wake the iPad. If that's too aggressive, tap the Require Passcode button and

choose a timing during which the passcode isn't needed after entering it successfully once.

Figure 11.2
Setting a passcode

6. If you don't want anyone seeing your photos in the Picture Frame mode, turn the Picture Frame mode to Off. The Picture Frame button no longer appears on the lock screen.

7. To give the passcode lock some more teeth, enable the Erase Data option. If an incorrect password is attempted 10 times, the iPad wipes its memory.

note After you set a passcode lock, you need to enter it whenever you want to make changes to the passcode settings.

note Although a Smart Cover will wake the iPad from sleep automatically when opened, it doesn't bypass the passcode lock. You still need to enter your code before using the iPad.

Use a VPN

When you connect to a public Wi-Fi hotspot, there's a real chance that someone could be analyzing traffic on the network. The way to protect against it (other than to choose not to use public Wi-Fi networks, but that's not a good option) is to set up a Virtual Private Network. A VPN establishes a secure connection to the Internet and protects your traffic from prying eyes.

Your employer may have provided you with VPN connection information, or you might prefer to pay for a service such as WiTopia (www.witopia.net). With the account information, configure the VPN settings so you can switch on the VPN when you need it.

1. Go to Settings > General > Network, and tap the Add VPN Configuration button.

2. Enter the server and settings provided to you (**Figure 11.3**).

Figure 11.3
VPN settings

3. Tap the Save button.

When you want to activate the VPN, return to Settings, where VPN now appears in the main Settings list; tap the VPN switch to On. After the connection is made and authenticated, a VPN icon appears in the status bar (**Figure 11.4**).

Figure 11.4
VPN indicator

VPN active —

The VPN settings screen keeps tabs on how long you've been connected; tapping the Status button also reveals more information, such as the VPN server name and the IP address assigned to your iPad.

When you no longer need the connection, tap the VPN switch to Off.

> **tip** The VPN connection will close when the iPad goes to sleep, so be sure to reestablish a link the next time you wake it up to maintain secure communications.

Set Up Usage Restrictions

One unsurprising trend I've seen since the iPad was released is that it's a device that gets shared—whether you intend it to be shared or not. A good friend bought an iPad just before leaving on vacation, and he quickly discovered that it makes a great traveling companion. His young son used it on the plane to play educational games and watch videos, and then his wife used it to read ebooks in the evenings. He was lucky to get his hands on the iPad late at night after everyone else went to bed.

The problem is that the iPad isn't set up like a Mac or Windows PC, which have the ability to host multiple separate accounts. So, for example, my friend's email messages were exposed to anyone who wanted to go looking (or accidentally deleting), and he wouldn't have been able to prevent the boy from stumbling onto Web sites inappropriate for a three-year-old.

That's where the iPad's Restrictions settings come in. They don't cover all possibilities—I'd like to see a future version of the operating system have a guest mode optimized for handing the iPad over to someone—but they do help prevent unwanted access.

1. Go to Settings > General > Restrictions to access the settings.

2. Tap the Enable Restrictions button.

3. Enter a Restrictions passcode in the keypad that appears, then enter it again for verification. This passcode is separate from the one you may have set up to lock the iPad.

4. In the first block of settings, determine which apps and services are allowed to run (**Figure 11.5**). When you switch an option to Off, the app disappears from the Home screen. When Location is disabled, the iPad doesn't share its location with apps that request it.

Figure 11.5
App restrictions

5. In the Allowed Content block of settings, choose which media can be viewed (**Figure 11.6**). For example, you may wish to limit videos to movies rated no higher than PG when the kids are awake, and then change the rating or disable restrictions when you want to watch something rated R after the kids have gone to bed.

Figure 11.6
Media restrictions

Allowed Content:	
Ratings For	United States >
Music & Podcasts	Explicit >
Movies	All >
TV Shows	All >
Apps	All >
In-App Purchases	ON

Use Find My iPad

Find My iPad can locate your iPad on a map (even the Wi-Fi–only model, provided it's connected to a hotspot), send sounds or messages to it, or remotely erase its data if you think you'll never see it again.

Set up Find My iPad

Do the following to make sure Find My iPad is active; you don't want to discover too late that you may not have set up the feature.

1. On the iPad, go to Settings > iCloud.

2. Set the Find My iPad option to On.

3. Tap Allow in the dialog that appears to grant the feature access to location data.

 note For Find My iPad to work, the Location Services option (in the General pane) must be turned on.

Take action on a lost iPad

Whether your iPad has fallen behind the back cushion on the couch or fallen into the wrong hands, you can take several actions using Find My iPad to help locate it.

 tip If you own another iOS device, like an iPhone, download the free Find My iPhone app to locate your devices.

- **Find:** In a Web browser, go to www.icloud.com and sign in. If necessary, click the navigation button at the upper-left corner of the screen to view the iCloud features, and click the Find My iPhone icon. (Apple uses "Find My iPhone" as a generic name, even if you're not looking for an iPhone.) After a minute or so, your iPad should appear on a map noting its location (**Figure 11.7**).

  Unless there's a solid fix on the iPad's signal, the location may not be accurate. After a few minutes, a better location is resolved. You can also click the Refresh Location (🔄) button to refresh the view, which is useful if the iPad seems to be on the move.

Figure 11.7
Find My iPad, found

Navigation button ─

iPad location ─

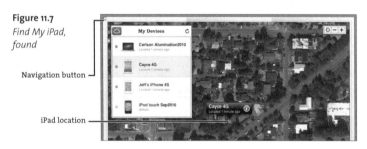

- **Play Sound or Send Message:** If you suspect you've simply misplaced the iPad in your home (where the top-down map wouldn't provide enough resolution), click the Info button (ⓘ) and then click the Play Sound or Send Message button. Enter a message and optionally slide the Play Sound switch to On (**Figure 11.8**). (The sound resembles a submarine's sonar ping and plays loud, whatever the iPad's volume setting.)

Figure 11.8
Find My iPad message being sent and received

> **tip** I was trying to be cute in the figure above, but if you think someone might have picked up the iPad, you could use the message feature to alert that the iPad is lost, offer a reward for its return, or just include a contact email or phone number.

- **Remote Lock:** Click the Info button (ⓘ) and then click Lock iPad to lock the iPad immediately (even if someone is in the middle of using the device) with the device's passcode.

- **Remote Wipe:** Click the Info button (ⓘ) and then click Wipe iPad if you think the iPad is gone for good or don't want to risk that someone may get past the passcode and access sensitive information (**Figure 11.9**).

Figure 11.9
Are you sure?

All data on the iPad is automatically hardware-encrypted, so technically, performing a remote wipe doesn't actually remove any data; it changes the encryption key, leaving the encrypted data useless. As a result, wiping is fast, taking only a minute and a half.

If the iPad does turn up after a remote wipe, connect it to your computer and restore everything from the last backup.

Encrypt iPad Backup

Speaking of the iPad's backup, you could perform remote wipes all day and it won't matter if the computer you sync with was stolen along with the iPad. You can get some measure of relief if you also encrypt the iPad data backup that's stored on the computer's hard disk.

In iTunes with the iPad selected in the sidebar, go to the Summary pane and enable the "Encrypt local backup" option.

12

Troubleshooting

As I write this, the iPad is barely two years old and in its third generation of hardware—quite young by technology standards. When something truly new comes out, not just an update to something long familiar, we expect to run into problems that the engineers could not have anticipated under lab conditions.

And yet, the iPad is surprisingly stable. Since receiving my original model on the first day they were available in the U.S., and now including my third-generation iPad, I've experienced maybe a few dozen application crashes and only occasional hard freezes that made the iPad unresponsive—all easily fixed. (Compare that to an average Mac or Windows PC.)

But that's the point, isn't it? It should all just work, and for most of the iPad experience, it does. When it doesn't, a few simple steps will solve the majority of problems that crop up.

Restart the iPad

I don't want to sound flip, but restarting the iPad is almost a universal cure-all. If the iPad's internal working memory gets full or fragmented, you may see problems or sluggish performance.

1. Press and hold the Sleep/Wake button on the case. A red slider labeled "Slide to power off" appears at the top of the screen.

2. Drag the slider. After a few seconds, the iPad turns off.

3. Count to 10, and then restart the iPad by pressing the Sleep/Wake button until the Apple logo appears.

When an App Crashes

The iOS, which runs the show, is designed so that if an app crashes, it does it without affecting other processes. A crashed app typically just disappears, at which point you'll find yourself back at the Home screen. Tap the app to launch it again and you should be fine.

If the problem persists, check for an update at the App Store. Also read the release notes for the app; developers must submit their apps to Apple for approval, and if a bug has crept in, there's a lag between when an updated version is submitted and when it becomes available.

If that doesn't work, delete the app from the iPad and reinstall it.

If an App Is Sluggish or Unresponsive

Sometimes an app can start to have problems, but not crash outright. In that case, you can force it to quit by doing the following:

1. Press the Home button to go to the Home screen (or switch to another app, as long as the troublemaking app isn't the one running).

2. Double-press the Home button, or swipe up with three or four fingers, to reveal the recents list.

3. Touch and hold the app until the icons begin to shake.

4. Tap the red button in the upper-left corner of the app's icon (**Figure 12.1**). The app quits immediately.

5. Press the Home button to exit the app editing mode.

Figure 12.1
Force-quitting an app

Tap to quit app.

Reinstall an App

If the copy of an app on the iPad has become corrupted for some reason, try a fresh copy.

1. On the iPad, touch and hold the app's icon until all of the icons begin to shake, then tap the Delete button (the X) to remove the app.

2. Perform a sync (either connected by cable or via Wi-Fi).

3. In the Apps pane within iTunes, locate the app and make sure it's enabled for syncing. When you delete an app from the iPad, you still have a backup version in iTunes.

4. Click the Apply button to re-sync and transfer the app back to the iPad.

If that doesn't solve the crashing problem, and it seems clear that other people are not having the same issue, try starting over with the app.

1. Delete the app from the iPad.

2. Also delete the app from iTunes: Click the Apps icon in the sidebar, locate the app in the list, and press Delete App. Verify that you want to remove the app (**Figure 12.2**), and in the next dialog choose to move the file to the Trash.

Figure 12.2
Deleting an app from iTunes

Are you sure you want to delete the selected app from your iTunes library?

This app will also be deleted from any iPod, iPhone, or iPad which synchronizes with your iTunes library.

☐ Do not ask me again

Cancel   Delete App

tip   To find an app in iTunes easily, switch to List view and then click the Kind column heading. Apps are then grouped by device, such as "iPad app" and "iPhone/iPod touch/iPad app." Or, start typing the name of an app in the iTunes Search field in the upper-right corner of the window.

3. Go to the App Store and tap Install (on the iPad) or Download (in iTunes) (**Figure 12.3**). Since you'd bought it previously, you aren't charged again.

Figure 12.3
Reinstall an app.

NYTimes for iPad
News
Updated Mar 15, 2012
256 Ratings
INSTALL

4. Sync the iPad if you downloaded the app from iTunes. If you downloaded it on the iPad, open the app.

Connectivity Issues

The iPad was designed to connect to the Internet over a wireless connection, so not having that connection can be frustrating. If you can't connect, try the following:

- Look for a connection indicator in the upper-left corner of the screen (**Figure 12.4**). The Wi-Fi icon appears when you're connected to a Wi-Fi network. If you're using a Wi-Fi–only iPad, the lack of the Wi-Fi icon means you have no connection. If you're using a cellular iPad, as shown here, the cellular network is active when Wi-Fi isn't available; you'll see LTE, 4G, or 3G, depending on model and available service.

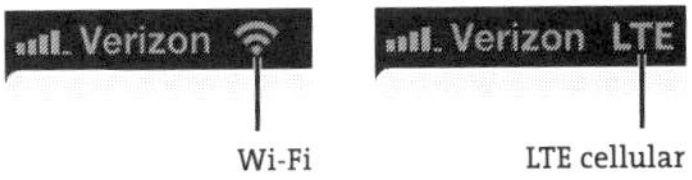

Figure 12.4
Wireless connection icons

Wi-Fi

LTE cellular

- On a cellular iPad, the network indicator icon and signal strength bars appear even if you haven't paid for an active data plan. If the signal is there but you can't get online, make sure you've activated a data plan or that you've not reached the limit of your data plan (see Chapter 1 for more information).

- Try turning off Wi-Fi and turning it back on again. In Settings > Wi-Fi, set the Wi-Fi switch to Off, wait a minute, and then set it back to On.

- Similarly, try turning off the cellular radio on a 4G iPad and then turning it back on. In Settings > Cellular Data, toggle the Cellular Data switch.

- In the Wi-Fi settings, tap the detail button (⊚) next to the name of the active network to view its advanced settings (**Figure 12.5**, on the next page). Then, tap the Renew Lease button, which makes the iPad request a new temporary IP address from the Wi-Fi base station.

Figure 12.5
Renewing the Wi-Fi network lease

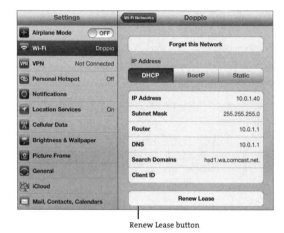

Renew Lease button

If the iPad Doesn't Appear in iTunes

The iPad needs to connect to iTunes, but sometimes that may not happen. Try these solutions, in order of least to most inconvenient:

- Make sure iTunes is up to date. On the Mac, go to the iTunes menu and choose Check for Updates. Under Windows, choose Check for Updates under the Help menu.

- Connect the iPad to a different USB port on your computer.

- Use a different sync cable.

- Restart the iPad and the computer.

- Download a new copy of iTunes (from www.apple.com/itunes/) and reinstall the software on the computer.

- If none of those suggestions work under Mac OS X, you may need to replace the Apple Mobile Device Service. Find detailed instructions in the following article: http://support.apple.com/kb/HT1747.

Battery Issues

The iPad's battery requires more power to charge than what many computers put out through their USB ports, which can be a shock to some people who buy the device, plug it into their computers, and see a Not Charging indicator in the status bar (**Figure 12.6**). Actually, the iPad *is* charging, but at a very low rate. If you left it asleep and connected overnight, you'd see more power than when you went to sleep. See "Charge the iPad battery" in Chapter 1 for more information.

Figure 12.6
Not Charging indicator

If battery life seems dramatically worse than it did when you bought the iPad, contact Apple about possibly getting a replacement under warranty.

If you're out of warranty and the iPad "requires service due to the battery's diminished ability to hold an electrical charge" (in Apple's words), then you can take advantage of Apple's battery replacement service. For $99, Apple will replace the entire iPad (so be sure you've synchronized it before sending it off). See www.apple.com/support/ipad/service/battery/ for more information.

Reset the iPad

If the iPad does not respond to input at all, it needs to be reset.

Press and hold the Sleep/Wake and Home buttons simultaneously for 10 seconds or until the Apple logo appears. Resetting does not erase the iPad's memory.

Restore the iPad to Factory Defaults

If you continue to have problems, or if you simply want to start over from scratch, you can restore the iPad to its initial state. Remember, this action erases your data from the iPad, so make sure you sync first (if the iPad is working properly) to back up your data.

1. Connect the iPad to your computer.

2. In iTunes, select the iPad in the sidebar and click the Restore button in the Summary pane.

3. In the confirmation dialog that appears, click the Restore button (**Figure 12.7**).

Figure 12.7
Restoring the iPad to its initial state

The first time you do this, iTunes downloads a clean version of the iPad's software; subsequent restores pull the data from your hard disk. In either case, you must have an active Internet connection, because iTunes verifies the iPad with Apple's servers.

4. Wait. iTunes copies the data to the iPad, which installs it. After a few minutes, the iPad is ready.

5. In iTunes, choose a backup to restore to the device. Or, you can opt to set it up as a new iPad with just the data that ships on it.

tip For more detailed options, see the following article at Apple's Web site: "iOS: Resolving update and restore alert messages" (http://support.apple.com/kb/TS1275).

Force the iPad into Recovery Mode

Although unlikely, the iPad may not even get to the point where you can select it in iTunes and restore the software. In that case, try forcing the iPad to load in its recovery mode:

1. Make sure that the sync cable is connected to your computer and that iTunes is running.

2. Press and hold the Home button.

3. Connect the sync cable to the iPad's dock connector.

The iPad should appear as if it were a new, empty device. Follow the steps on the previous page to restore the software.

Index